IRA

LIPMAN

UNITED STATES
ATTORNEY

ALSO BY WHITNEY NORTH SEYMOUR, JR.

Why Justice Fails

The Young Die Quietly:
The Narcotics Problem in America

Small Urban Spaces (Editor)

UNITED STATES ATTORNEY

AN INSIDE VIEW OF "JUSTICE" IN AMERICA
UNDER THE NIXON ADMINISTRATION

by Whitney North Seymour, Jr.

WILLIAM MORROW AND COMPANY, INC.
NEW YORK   1975

Printed in the United States of America.
1 2 3 4 5 79 78 77 76 75

Library of Congress Cataloging in Publication Data

Seymour, Whitney North (date)
    United States Attorney.

    1. Criminal justice, Administration of—United States.
2. Attorneys-general—United States. 3. Law enforcement—
United States. I. Title.
KF9223.S44   353.5   75-16289
ISBN 0-688-02945-0

Dedicated to Assistant United States Attorneys—past, present and future—who provide the idealism, integrity, and independence of Federal law enforcement.

ACKNOWLEDGMENTS

The reasons for writing this book are many. The first is to record events in an important and troubled period in the history of this nation, and in particular in the history of Federal law enforcement. The second is to improve the administration of Federal criminal justice by fostering a better understanding of the key role played by the United States Attorney, and of the peculiar strengths and weaknesses of the present system. The third is to correct a number of false impressions that have crept into the public domain because of erroneous and, too often, biased news reporting. The fourth, and most important, is to encourage adherence to standards of excellence and integrity by the young men and women who may in the future serve in United States Attorneys' offices or other government agencies.

Although every book is ultimately the responsibility of its author, this one is to a large extent the joint product of many hands. Among those to whom I am most indebted in the endeavor are the following: my friends Agnes Marquette and Reta Thompson, who typed the manuscript with unflagging interest, intelligence, and enthusiasm; my elder daughter, Tryntje, who pressed me into writing the book in the first place; Catryna and Gabriel, who cheerfully helped see me through the process despite the loss of precious weekends and vacation time; my editor, Hillel Black, whose perception and good taste have given the book direction; Elizabeth Otis, whose enthusiasm as my literary agent has sustained me now through three books; and Harold Baer, Jr., Mike Hess, Bob Morvillo, and Jim Rayhill, who patiently checked the manuscript and contributed so much to the book's substance through their own work in the office.

Special thanks go to Anthony P. Grech, librarian of the Association of the Bar of the City of New York, who helped me find much of the historical material that provides the basis for the first chapter. I am also indebted for historical material to the splendid Scoville Memorial Library, in Salisbury, Connecticut. John S. Marsh, talented legal scholar and librarian, generously volunteered his considerable skills in the preparation of the index, for which I am most grateful.

Finally, I express my gratitude to those who were responsible for my appointment as United States Attorney, although apparently I turned out to be something of a surprise—especially to the White House. In the spring of 1973, there was a brief reference to my activities as United States Attorney in the course of one of the taped conversations in the Oval Office. One of President Nixon's top advisers disdainfully referred to me on that occasion as a "softheaded do-gooder." I accept the accusation with pride.

W.N.S., JR.

CONTENTS

There is no other public office which makes such a direct and inspiring call upon the conscience and professional zeal of a high-minded lawyer as that office, or in which courageous effort and steady poise bring such a sense of satisfaction to the occupant.

—HENRY L. STIMSON,
in a letter to Martin Conboy
upon the latter's appointment as
United States Attorney for the
Southern District of New York (1933)

INTRODUCTION

I had the unique but not enviable experience of serving as United States Attorney under two Attorneys General of the United States who were later convicted for serious crimes involving corruption in government and obstruction of justice. To me fell the unpleasant duty of supervising the investigation and indictment of one of those Attorneys General for perjury and conspiracy to obstruct justice. During this period of moral eclipse in the top leadership of the Department of Justice, I also had a chance to observe and work with a number of fellow United States Attorneys who, by contrast, demonstrated the highest standards of honesty, independence, and professionalism in the running of their own districts. Among these were Frederick Lacey and Herbert Stern, in Newark, who broke the stranglehold of organized crime on local municipal government in a number of New Jersey communities; James Thompson, of Chicago, who ran the gauntlet of criticism while unearthing widespread corruption in state and local administration and election machinery; George Beall, of Baltimore, who had the unique distinction of indicting the Vice-President of

11

the United States for income-tax evasion; and Richard Thornburgh, of Pittsburgh, who was one of the pioneers in gaining environmental protection through the courts. There were others as well. The accomplishments of these men, together with the achievements in our own district, are not only splendid tributes to the character and ability of the people involved. More importantly, they demonstrate the capacity of the Federal justice system to provide fair and effective enforcement of the law.

I was inducted as United States Attorney on January 16, 1970, and served for three and a half years, until June 1, 1973. During that time I supervised a staff of over ninety Assistant United States Attorneys and another hundred civil service employees, all engaged in the broad spectrum of Federal law enforcement, both criminal and civil. I was assisted by a remarkable team: Silvio J. Mollo, Chief Assistant United States Attorney, who had joined the staff as a very young man and was completing his thirty-fourth year at the time of my own departure; Harold Baer, Jr., First Assistant United States Attorney and chief of the Criminal Division, a talented lawyer and investigator with unique insight into the human problems of defendants, witnesses, and others caught up in the criminal justice process; James W. Rayhill, who possessed one of the rarest of human qualities, kindness, even in the most difficult and trying times, and as a result was able to inspire members of the staff to perform at two or three times ordinary capacity; Michael D. Hess, a brilliant, loyal, and enthusiastic lawyer, whose creative approach to the law opened up many new frontiers; and Robert G. Morvillo, who succeeded Harold Baer as chief of the Criminal Division, and who provided special courtroom skill, tenacity, and an uncanny sense of fair play. Probably the most remarkable executive member, however, was my own secretary, Hester B. Coe, who had worked for years with A. Bruce Bielaski, the first head of the Bureau of Investigation in the Department of Justice, and had joined my staff when I was chief counsel of a special unit of the New York State Commission of Investigation, conducting investigations into municipal waste and corruption. Mrs. Coe was at the center of operations for the Southern District of New York—she screened all sensitive mail; served as goodwill ambassador with other government agencies and members of the public; handled important telephone calls with monastic discretion; and was a thoughtful friend to the young lawyers on the staff.

I first become familiar with the United States Attorney's office for the Southern District of New York shortly after I graduated from law school and started practice in a large Manhattan law firm. My goal was to become a trial lawyer, but I found that in a Wall Street law office the courtroom opportunities were very slim. The cases usually involved large sums of money and were therefore handled only by the firm's partners, while the young lawyers carried the briefcases and did the legal research. Two and a half years after I started practicing law, President Dwight D. Eisenhower named J. Edward Lumbard, a leading trial lawyer, as United States Attorney for the Southern District of New York. Judge Lumbard started recruiting Assistants for his staff by requesting recommendations from the senior litigation partners in the larger firms. I heard about the opportunity and applied for the position for the express purpose of gaining trial experience. I was part of the first group of six Assistant U. S. Attorneys sworn in by Judge Lumbard after he took office. I spent three and a half years in the Criminal Division, participating in a number of criminal jury trials and in the successful income-tax prosecution of gangster Frank Costello. In time, I became Chief Appellate Attorney. Meanwhile, Judge Lumbard was nominated for appointment to the Second Circuit Court of Appeals, the most important appellate court in the country after the Supreme Court. When Judge Lumbard called the staff together to announce his departure, he spoke to us along the following lines:

> You young men and women have had every opportunity that our society can provide—good homes, good

13

family life, good educations, and an opportunity to taste public service in one of the greatest public law offices in the country. Soon you will be leaving to return to private practice or other pursuits. When you do, I urge you to get involved in politics. Do not stand aloof because you believe politics is a dirty business. It will only be dirty if people like you are unwilling to participate. With the opportunities you have had, you have an obligation to take an active part in our political process and to insure that it works well.

Within a week after I resigned from the U. S. Attorney's office in 1956, I walked over to my local Republican club, in Greenwich Village. It was the first time I had ever been in the place. I began ringing doorbells as a district captain, and was in time rewarded by nomination to run for the State Assembly. Although the race was hopeless, it brought me to the attention of the staff of the newly-elected Governor, Nelson Rockefeller, who named me chief counsel to a temporary state commission investigating municipal wrongdoing. In 1965, I again ran for the legislature, this time for the State Senate, and won. After three enjoyable but frustrating years in Albany I ran for Congress in 1968, but was defeated in the fallout from that year's large anti-Republican vote in New York City.

My appointment a few months later as United States Attorney was almost an accident. I was not the party nominee for the post. In fact, I had little political support because of my independent stand when I had served in the state legislature. But through my bar association activities I had developed friendships with a number of leading lawyers at the New York Bar, including many who themselves had good political credentials. When several friends urged me to seek the post of United States Attorney, I called on these senior lawyers and asked for their help. Several were former public officials; some had even served as U. S. Attorney. What I asked each of them was simply to write a letter on my behalf to whomever they knew best in the new Administration. Which ones did write, and to whom, I do not know to this day, but it was not long before I received a telephone call asking me to come to Washington for an interview with the Deputy Attorney General, whom I had never met. (I had not met the Attorney General or the President either, for that matter.) Several days later, the Deputy called to tell me I had been selected for the job. I still find it hard to believe. I went right up to the courthouse to inform the incumbent, Robert M. Morgenthau, and to discuss a timetable for transition. On January 16, 1970, I was sworn in.

Toward the end of my service as United States Attorney I put down in writing and gave to each Assistant a statement of what I believed it meant to be an Assistant United States Attorney in the Southern District of New York. The text reflected my own strong convictions about the goals and traditions of the office.

> To be an Assistant United States Attorney for the Southern District of New York is a badge of honor that must be earned not once, but three times. First, by being selected out of a large field of outstanding candidates on the basis of one's own merits. Once more, by hard work in developing personal discipline, professional skills, independent judgment, and total dedication to the public interest. And finally, by keeping alive the traditions, friendships, and high principles of the office over the course of future years.
>
> To be an Assistant United States Attorney for the Southern District of New York requires commitment to absolute integrity and fair play; to candor and fairness in dealing with adversaries and the courts; to careful preparation, not making any assumptions or leaving anything to chance; and to never proceeding in any case unless convinced of the guilt of the accused or the correctness of one's position.
>
> To be an Assistant United States Attorney for the Southern District of New York demands unusual personal qualities—promptness, dependability, precision, thoughtfulness, decency, personal courage, and conviction.
>
> One's basic credo should agree with Thomas Paine's:

"The world is my country, all mankind are my brethren, and to do good is my religion."

When the time came for me to return to private practice, I met with the legal staff for a final time. The following paragraphs are written from my notes of what I said on that occasion. I repeat them here because they distill what I believe to be the essence of the tradition of the Southern District of New York. I hope they may be of help to others in their own careers.

The following rules of personal conduct provide the key to success, whether in public service, in one's profession, or in private life.

1. *Do it now.* Every job is easier if it is done promptly, without procrastination. "The leading rule for the lawyer, as for the man of every other calling," wrote Lincoln, "is diligence. Leave nothing for tomorrow which can be done today."

2. *Don't be a talker, be a doer.* Of all the qualities in human beings, *dependability* is the most important. The worst defect is to be constantly talking about what one is *going* to do, or looking for excuses for not having done it.

3. *Think of the other fellow.* The most effective way to achieve good working relationships is to take a little time to show an interest in the other person as a human being. Ask him about his family, his activities, his vacation plans. Concentrate on being thoughtful and helpful to others. When you answer the telephone, or greet a visitor, your first words should be "How can I help you?" or "What can I do for you?"

4. *Be sure to communicate clearly.* Most of the disputes between human beings result from a breakdown in communications. One of the most important responsibilities of a lawyer is to keep his clients advised about important developments. In government, it is equally important to keep all officials who have a legitimate interest in what you are doing fully informed. Stop and think: who should be kept posted? And when you do inform them, be clear and specific.

5. *Do what* you *believe is* right. Do not be afraid of making a mistake, as long as you believe you are doing the right thing. In the words of Theodore Roosevelt, "Show me a man who doesn't make mistakes, and I will show you a man who doesn't get things done."

6. *Above all, be independent.* Stand on your own two feet. Do not worry about what other people will say. Worry about your own conscience. Follow the rule of public service articulated by Abraham Lincoln over a century ago:

> I desire so to conduct the affairs of this administration that if at the end, when I come to lay down the reins of power, I have lost every other friend on earth, I shall at least have one friend left, and that friend shall be down inside of me.

WHITNEY NORTH SEYMOUR, JR.

1

THE MAKING OF
THE DEPARTMENT OF JUSTICE

In 1924, President Calvin Coolidge invited his Amherst class-mate Harlan Fiske Stone, former dean of Columbia Law School, to come to see him at the White House. The President told Stone he had nominated him to be Attorney General of the United States. As he left the meeting with the President, Stone approached a police sergeant stationed outside the White House. "Where," he asked, "is the Justice Department?"

People do not need to ask that question anymore. The Department of Justice has become one of the most formidable agencies in the Federal Government. But fifty years ago it was a different story. The Department had only been in existence since 1870. Before that time virtually all legal matters on behalf of the Government had been handled by the United States Attorneys, on the local-district level.

The position of Attorney General in this country was inherited from the British legal system. When the legal profession first came into being, during the reign of Edward I, in the thirteenth century, certain members were designated "Crown Attorneys" to protect the royal privileges in the courts. By the time of Edward IV, in the mid-fifteenth century, the title for this function had changed to Attorney General. In England, the Attorney General provided advice to the King and his ministers and conducted public prosecutions in major criminal cases. The office was first established in the American colonies when Richard Lee was appointed Attorney General for Virginia, in 1643. Rhode Island named its first Attorney General in 1650. The Connecticut Assembly provided for a similar office in 1704, specifying that the post required "a sober, discreet and religious person."

Two major differences developed between the offices of Attorney General in England and America. In Great Britain, most criminal cases were instituted by private counsel retained by the injured victim, with the Attorney General's participation limited to cases of state significance instituted at the direction of the King. England, in fact, did not establish a Director of Public Prosecutions until 1879. In the colonies, meanwhile, private prosecutions were abandoned as a law-enforcement technique. The Connecticut statute enacted in 1704 provided that a public prosecutor should be appointed in each county "to suppresse vice and immoralitie." By the end of the eighteenth century, official prosecutions of criminal cases had become the norm under the American system of justice. To a large extent this reliance on public prosecutors reflected the influence of the French legal system, with its *avocat général* and *procurer du roi*, who by the seventeenth century had taken over local criminal prosecutions in France.

Unlike the English Attorney General, the American counterpart began to emerge as an important political figure. In England, political and court administrative functions were vested in the office of the Lord Chancellor, who presided over the House of Lords. The English Attorney General remained essentially independent of the political policies of the administration in power. In contrast, both Federal and state Attorneys General in the United States tended to be intimately tied in with the programs and policies of the President or Governor.

Contrary to popular assumption, the Attorney General of the United States does not hold a constitutional office. The post was created by act of Congress and it can be changed at any time, simply by passing a new statute.

THE FIRST ONE HUNDRED YEARS

The Constitution of the United States provided that the judicial power be vested in a Supreme Court "and in such inferior courts as the Congress may from time to time ordain and establish." In 1789 Congress adopted the Judiciary Act, which created the Federal court system. The statute also created the office of Attorney General, but limited his powers to the conduct of cases in the Supreme Court in which the United States was interested, and to the giving of legal opinions when requested by the President and the heads of executive departments. Congress protected against centralization of Federal legal power by providing that all Federal criminal and civil cases in the lower courts be handled on a district-by-district basis by United States Attorneys appointed by the President for that purpose. The law enforcement responsibility was thus given to the *local* Federal attorneys, and the Attorney General was expressly excluded from any direct control of litigation except when cases reached the Supreme Court.

From the beginning, the Attorney General was treated as something of a stepchild by the Federal Government. His salary was only fifteen hundred dollars a year, half of the sum paid to other cabinet members. He was not expected to work full time, and, in fact, his low salary was fixed in expectation that he would supplement it through private practice. He had no office or staff or funds to pay expenses. President Madison sent a message to Congress urging that body to correct the situation, but Congress did not act. In 1818, President Monroe finally persuaded Congress to authorize the employment of the first clerk to assist the Attorney General, and in 1819 Congress appropriated five hundred dollars for the clerk's office expenses. The Attorney General had no official quarters until 1822, when he was given a small room in the War Department Building. In 1831, Congress authorized a modest appropriation to buy some law books, and in 1850 approved the hiring of an additional clerk. The Attorney General's office at mid-century had a staff totaling exactly four people: the Attorney General himself, two clerks, and a messenger. By the time of the Civil War, the staff had expanded to include two legal assistants and four permanent clerks.

The Civil War finally provided the impetus for centralizing Federal law enforcement, and in 1861 Congress passed a law giving the Attorney General the power to supervise and direct the United States Attorneys and United States Marshals in the various districts. A single Federal law-enforcement agency was created in 1870, when Congress passed a statute establishing the Department of Justice and providing for a Solicitor General and three Assistant Attorneys General. This legislation created the framework for the Department as we know it today. It gave the Attorney General supervision of the legal officers in various executive departments as well as control over all Federal criminal prosecutions and civil actions.

THE DEVELOPMENT OF FEDERAL LAW ENFORCEMENT MACHINERY

The original view of Federal law enforcement was extremely restricted. Most prosecutions of crime were to be handled by local prosecutors in the state courts. Federal prosecutors would be limited to matters of clear Federal concern. The first Federal criminal statute, passed by Congress in 1790, listed only the following as Federal crimes: treason; murder in a U. S. fort, an arsenal, or a dockyard; murder on the high seas; piracy; forging of U. S. currency and bonds; and bribery or obstruction of justice in the U. S. courts. In the preceding year, Congress had established the first Federal law enforcement agency, the Revenue Cutter Service, to try to reduce smuggling. Then, over the course of years, both Federal jurisdiction and Federal resources began to expand. Even so, as late as 1929 Federal jurisdiction over criminal cases was still extremely limited. A report to Congress in that year summarized Federal criminal statutes as: treason and sedition; crimes against the Government, election laws, civil rights, the postal service, and foreign and interstate commerce; and offenses committed within the territorial jurisdiction of the United States or on the high seas (including, among other things, polygamy and engaging in prizefights or bullfights).

Originally, the United States Marshals, created under the Judiciary Act of 1789, served as the sole arresting officers in Federal criminal cases. The position became a hazardous one with the opening of the Indian territories in the West. By the end of the nineteenth century, United States Marshals were being shot down at the rate of twenty a year in the pursuit of their dangerous calling. The exploits of these Federal officers have been recorded in romanticized form in western movies and television programs. Thereafter the role of the Marshal as a "law man" began to decline. Today his principal functions are holding people in detention, serving subpoenas and civil summonses, and providing some protective services for government witnesses. The U. S. Marshal no longer performs any investigative function.

Congress in 1836 created the first full-fledged Federal criminal investigative unit by authorizing the Postmaster General to hire agents to look into offenses involving the U. S. mails.

Shortly after the creation of the new Department of Justice, in 1870, came the first congressional appropriation for the Attorney General to detect and prosecute Federal offenses. At the time, there were numerous enforcement problems growing out of Reconstruction activities in the South, and Attorney General

Amos T. Akerman, the first head of the new Department, asked the Secret Service in the Treasury Department to provide investigators to assist with these prosecutions. In 1875, Attorney General George H. Williams appointed four special detectives for the Department, who were assigned to specific geographical areas. Occasionally thereafter the Department authorized local U. S. Attorneys to hire agents to investigate special cases.

Shortly after President Theodore Roosevelt came into office, in 1901, he learned of numerous frauds connected with the sale of public lands in the West. The Secretary of the Interior, suspecting that some of his own people were involved in the land frauds, asked that the Department of Justice conduct an investigation. The Attorney General borrowed Secret Service agents from the Treasury Department, and the resulting investigation produced sensational charges of wholesale criminal conduct, including involvement by a United States Senator and Congressman in a conspiracy to defraud. With its usual perspicacity, the Congress promptly passed a law *prohibiting* the Department of Justice from using Secret Service agents or any other investigators borrowed from outside agencies as "spies."

Roosevelt met the problem with characteristic bluntness. He directed Attorney General Charles J. Bonaparte to organize an investigative service *within* the Department of Justice which would report to no one except the Attorney General. Bonaparte issued a departmental order on July 26, 1908, creating the Bureau of Investigation, the forerunner of today's FBI.

EARLY GLIMPSES OF FEDERAL JUSTICE

The early history of Federal law enforcement was frequently colorful, but not always a cause for civic pride. One of the most dubious examples of Federal criminal jurisprudence took place immediately following the Civil War, when Mary Suratt, the keeper of a lodging house, was convicted along with other alleged conspirators on charges of being an accomplice to John Wilkes Booth in the assassination of Abraham Lincoln. The Secretary of War, Edward Stanton, had ordered military officers to investigate Lincoln's murder immediately after his death, and Mrs. Suratt had been held in prison while she was interrogated relentlessly by Col. Lafayette Baker. The Secretary of War announced that the trial of the co-conspirators would be conducted by a military commission rather than before a jury in a regular criminal trial. The Attorney General, James Speed, quickly accepted the decision and rendered an official opinion that the co-conspirators could properly be tried by a military commission since the crime had been committed in time of war against the Commander-in-chief of the military forces. The Attorney General apparently was not troubled by the fact that up until that time the regular civilian courts of the District of Columbia had handled all criminal cases.

Stanton proceeded to pack the commission with friends and personal appointees and brought the defendants to trial in less than a month. Mrs. Suratt was assigned as counsel two young lawyers with limited experience. To his considerable credit, former Attorney General Reverdy Johnson volunteered his services. Johnson had interviewed Mrs. Suratt and believed she was innocent of any knowing complicity in the assassination plot. Johnson's participation was challenged by the commission, whose legal authority he vehemently attacked. Thereafter he played a minor role in the proceedings to avoid prejudicing his client's case. The commission returned its verdict of guilty on June 30, 1865, condemning Mrs. Suratt and three of her co-defendants to death, and three others to life imprisonment. One other co-defendant was sentenced to six years. On July 5, President Andrew Johnson signed an order approving the sentences. The hangings were scheduled to take place two days later.

Mrs. Suratt's lawyers applied to the District of Columbia courts for a writ of habeas corpus, which was issued returnable at 10 A.M. on July 7. The military officer having custody of the defendant appeared in court and (through his lawyer, the Attorney General of the United States) announced that he would *not* comply with the writ. His reason was that an order had been issued by the President of the United States that very morning declaring that the writ of habeas corpus was suspended. The hanging of the co-conspirators took place immediately.

Days later, the Supreme Court of the United States, in the landmark case of *Ex parte Milligan,* held that a military tribunal could not usurp the functions of regular civilian courts when they were in operation, but the decision came too late to help Mrs. Suratt, who became the first woman ever to be executed under Federal law.

Later it became known that five members of the nine-man military commission had recommended leniency for Mrs. Suratt but that Secretary Stanton had not communicated the mercy recommendation to President Johnson at the time he submitted the report of the court-martial. Consequently, President Johnson ordered Stanton to resign. Stanton refused and was dismissed. (President Ulysses S. Grant later appointed Stanton to the Supreme Court. Fate, however, intervened, and Stanton died within the week of his appointment.)

Among the remarkable personalities identified with early Federal law enforcement was Alan Pinkerton, son of a Scottish police sergeant, who had been hired by the Post Office Department as one of its special agents in the early middle of the nineteenth century, but who soon decided that he could do better running his own private detective agency. In 1851, he organized Pinkerton's National Detective Agency, which became one of the principal investigative instruments for the railroads, which were being harassed by train robberies and freight thefts. Pinkerton operated under an unusual code of ethics, which ruled out any investigations in divorce cases or into the background of jurors. None of his employees was permitted to accept rewards. His trademark was a human eye superimposed with the words "We Never Sleep"—whence the expression "private eye."

Another colorful Federal investigator during the early years was William J. Burns, a Secret Service agent who became famous for his work in tracking down counterfeiters. Burns worked on the land-fraud cases that led Congress to prohibit the use of Secret Service agents by the Justice Department. Burns was lent to the civic leaders of San Francisco when they petitioned President Theodore Roosevelt for assistance in investigating municipal corruption. Using a peephole in the office wall of a cooperating skating-rink proprietor, Burns took careful notes while city officials were paid bribes in marked currency to vote against a proposed ordinance to outlaw commercial recreational enterprises. Three officials were thus trapped, and they in turn provided information leading to major prosecutions and reforms in the scandal-ridden city. In 1909, Burns resigned from Federal service and organized the private-detective agency that still bears his name.

Because of the lack of adequate national law enforcement protection, the railroads were forced to establish their own private police forces during the late nineteenth century. The railroad detectives produced many fabled law enforcement figures, including Daniel J. O'Connell, who spent a lifetime working for the Southern Pacific Railroad, which was the principal passenger and freight carrier in the Western states and a regular prey of bandits from the day of its very first run. O'Connell solved most of the Southern Pacific's holdups through his own diligent hard work. He was also a man of considerable personal courage, and won wide respect for walking into a saloon one day in 1921 and single-handedly capturing Roy Gardner, "the king of escape artists," who had twice previously jumped from moving trains while under arrest. O'Connell walked up to the table where Gardner was playing cards and ordered him to put up his hands. He then simply locked a pair of handcuffs around Gardner's wrists and led his quarry away. By the time he retired, O'Connell headed a private police force of nearly a thousand men, performing a job that Federal agents simply could not handle.

THE EARLY TWENTIETH CENTURY

On February 23, 1902, J. P. Morgan called on President Theodore Roosevelt. Morgan was agitated. Four days before, Philander C. Knox, Roosevelt's Attorney General, had announced that the Government was about to file an antitrust action to force dissolution of the Northern Securities Company. The New Jersey holding company had been organized a few months before to establish a railroad monopoly in the northwestern United States by combining the Union Pacific and Great Northern railroads.

"If we have done anything wrong," Mr. Morgan said, "send your man [the Attorney General] to my man [naming one of his lawyers] and they can fix it up."

"We don't want to fix it up," Attorney General Knox replied. "We want to stop it."

And stop it they did. Only a few years before, the Supreme Court had dismissed a case that had attempted to break up a monopoly in sugar production. This time, however, the Supreme Court held, by a 5-to-4 vote on March 10, 1904, that the Northern Securities Company *was* in violation of the antitrust laws. The case signaled the entry of the Department of Justice into trust-busting in a big way. For decades, big business had regarded the Federal courts and the Department of Justice as their allies. Now, for the first time, Federal law enforcement was beginning to show some muscle.

Twenty-five enforcement proceedings were instituted under the Sherman Antitrust Act during the days of the Roosevelt Administration, and another forty-five proceedings followed during Taft's regime. The Standard Oil Company and the American Tobacco Company, which had accumulated huge holdings and immense corporate power, were ordered to dissolve. Some years later, when Theodore Roosevelt returned from an African big-game hunting expedition and was honored with a parade up lower Broadway in Manhattan, John D. Rockefeller reportedly directed that no flags should be flown from Standard Oil's headquarters building at 26 Broadway. A heartfelt tribute.

The arrival of World War I presented a new kind of challenge to Federal law enforcement. For the first time, the Federal Government had to cope with organized espionage and sabotage activities, and also police a new nationwide draft of young men for military service. At the beginning of the war, the Federal agencies concerned with intelligence operations included small units in the Army and Navy; a section in the State Department; the Secret Service, which also had the responsibility of protecting the life of the President; and the Bureau of Investigation in the Department of Justice. The Bureau had only three hundred agents when war came, and soon found itself facing the impossible job of policing enemy aliens, protecting harbors and war industries, and aiding draft boards, in addition to its regular enforcement work. The German Government took full advantage of these weaknesses and set up a well-financed espionage and sabotage apparatus under the direct supervision of the German Embassy in Washington. The embassy's naval attaché organized a program of sabotaging ships carrying arms to the allies. Its military attaché, Franz von Papen, took charge of espionage and sabotage in the United States and Canada. The climax of the von Papen operation was a mammoth explosion on Black Tom Island in New York Harbor on July 30, 1916, which shattered windows in Jersey City, Manhattan, and Brooklyn and destroyed large stores of munitions. Other successful German espionage and sabotage operations resulted in a series of blasts in powder plants, warehouses, chemical plants, war factories, and ammunition dumps. Incendiary devices caused the burning of a number of American supply ships en route to England, France, and Russia.

After Congress declared war against Germany, in April, 1917, the workload for Federal law enforcement forces was increased even further with the mandatory registration of all enemy aliens and the problem of a climbing rate of military desertions. A. Bruce Bielaski, chief of the Bureau of Investigation, developed an ingenious method for expanding his agency by forming a volunteer organization affiliated with the Department of Justice—the American Protective League, which numbered 250,000 members at its peak. Unfortunately, this large number of volunteers made training and supervision difficult, with the result that a number of the members of the APL indulged their enthusiasm at the expense of the civil rights of the alleged violators. By the war's end, in 1918, the Federal Government had learned a good deal about the need for professionalism in its intelligence and anti-sabotage operations. In addition, passage of the Federal Espionage Act of 1917 imposed new sanctions against wartime and peacetime sabotage and espionage activities designed to aid enemy powers.

Following World War I, Federal law enforcement faced still another challenge—the Red Scare. The anarchist threat was literally dumped on the doorstep of the Attorney General of the United States. At 11:15 P.M. on June 2, 1919, a bomb exploded on the front stoop of A. Mitchell Palmer's home on R Street in Georgetown. The explosion shattered the front of the house and destroyed the library. A grisly fragment of the body of one of the bombers who was caught in the blast landed on the doorstep of the Assistant Secretary of the Navy, Franklin D. Roosevelt, who lived across the street. The Palmers had retired for the night to the second floor of their house, and were unharmed. But the reverberations from that explosion, together with eight other bomb blasts in other American cities on the same evening, caused waves of apprehension and resentment throughout the country. Bombs had been delivered to cabinet members, U. S. Senators and Congressmen, a Supreme Court Justice, a U. S. District Judge, two Governors, and several Wall Street figures. Federal law enforcement seemed to be paralyzed in the face of these assaults. A resolution was duly introduced in the United

States Senate demanding an explanation for the failure of the Department of Justice to take appropriate action to punish and deport those who advocated the overthrow of the Government by force and violence.

The following year a horse-drawn wagon halted next to J. P. Morgan's office on Wall Street. A bomb concealed in the rear of the wagon was detonated, killing thirty persons, wounding three hundred others, and leaving deep pockmarks on the side of the building which are still visible today. The Department of Justice now began to move in earnest. Searching for some legal authority to justify his actions, Attorney General Palmer focused attention on a statute that authorized deportation of any aliens who advocated violent overthrow of the Government. With the initial cooperation of the Labor Department, which issued hundreds of warrants against members of the Federation of the Union of Russian Workers, Department of Justice agents rounded up over two hundred officers and members in twelve cities. "Palmer's Red Raids" then picked up momentum. The Attorney General established a General Intelligence Division in the Department to study subversive activities. Placed in charge of the new unit was a twenty-four-year-old Special Assistant. On the basis of memoranda prepared by the youthful chief of the General Intelligence Division, Palmer ordered raids on the meeting places of the Communist Party of America and the Communist Labor Party. The young Special Assistant who planned the raids would one day be known to millions of his countrymen. His name was J. Edgar Hoover.

Based on Hoover's memoranda, a coordinated series of raids took place in thirty-three different cities on the evening of Friday, January 2, 1920. Twenty-five hundred aliens were rounded up and held for deportation hearings. The public outcry against the tactics used in the Palmer raids was immediate. Newspapers, lawyers, labor leaders, and members of Congress protested against the Department's invasion of meeting places and homes without search warrants, the wholesale arrest and detention of hundreds of individuals, and the abrogation of their right to counsel. During subsequent hearings in Congress, Attorney General Palmer publicly attacked the Assistant Secretary of Labor, who refused to order deportation of many of those who had been arrested. Palmer accused him of offering "protection and tolerance for the anarchists." Dean Stone of Columbia Law School, later to become Attorney General and then Chief Justice of the United States, openly urged the enactment of legislation to give aliens due-process protection against the "arbitrary exercise of power." The most serious result, however, was that the Communist Party promptly went underground.

The Department of Justice's decline in public confidence continued after the inauguration of President Warren G. Harding, in 1921, and his appointment of Harry N. Daugherty as Attorney General of the United States. Attorney General Daugherty immediately named William J. Burns, who had developed a seamy reputation for some of his past investigative activities, to become head of the Department's Bureau of Investigation. One of Burns's early appointments was Gaston B. Means, a detective who conducted confidential investigations on behalf of the Attorney General. Later Means bragged that he had organized espionage activities against a number of members of the United States Senate. Means spent considerable time with a shadowy figure named Jess Smith, who did not hold any official government post but had a private office in the Department of Justice and shared an apartment with the Attorney General at the Wardman Park Hotel. Jess Smith often appeared at White House social affairs and began to develop a wide reputation as a government fixer. With the revelation of scandals involving the Administration, Smith committed suicide in the Daugherty apartment. Senator Burton K. Wheeler sponsored a resolution calling for a Senate investigation into Attorney General Daugherty's conduct in office, but the Senator was himself indicted on charges brought on the basis of a Department of Justice investigation. Wheeler was later acquitted, and a Senate committee found him totally innocent. The inevitable conclusion was that the prosecution had been a vindictive countermove to halt the Senate investigation. Following President Harding's death, Calvin Coolidge demanded Daugherty's resignation.

Meanwhile, another Senate committee had initiated investigations into the leasing of naval oil-reserve properties to the mammoth Sinclair Oil Company, controlled by Harry F. Sinclair, and the Pan-American Petroleum & Transport Company, controlled by Edward L. Doheny. After months of preliminary skirmishing, it was disclosed that the Secretary of the Navy had transferred jurisdiction over the valuable oil properties to Albert B. Fall, the Secretary of the Interior. Fall had been a colleague of President Harding's when both served in the U. S. Senate. Secretary Fall had secretly signed leases permitting the Sinclair and Doheny companies to drill oil on the Federal reserve in return for a nominal royalty payment. He justified the leasing as necessary to protect against drainage of the oil reserves in the Teapot Dome through adjoining private wells, a theory that was later repudiated by petroleum experts. Fall claimed the absence of competitive bidding on the leases was in the national interest. He said he did not want Japan to learn the U. S. was stockpiling oil to operate its battle fleets. In time, it developed that Doheny had given Fall a hundred thousand dollars in cash, delivered by his son, and that Sinclair had provided additional sums in the form of Liberty Bonds.

Both houses of Congress passed a resolution calling on the President to appoint "special counsel" to institute civil and criminal proceedings against those responsible for the improper lease arrangements. The special counsel won a cancellation of the oil leases in the courts but did not fare as well in the criminal prosecutions. Both Doheny and Sinclair were acquitted of bribery, although Albert B. Fall was convicted and ultimately sentenced to a year in prison. Sinclair was sentenced to nine months for obstruction of justice arising out of his having the jurors in his first trial shadowed. The Teapot Dome scandal gave the nation full warning that the Department of Justice could be partisan in its enforcement of the law and that businessmen could successfully corrupt top Federal officials.

THE NOT-SO-GREAT EXPERIMENT

Prohibition provided another unhappy chapter in Federal law enforcement. The Volstead Act, passed in 1919, originally provided that enforcement of the anti-drinking law was to be the responsibility of the Commissioner of Internal Revenue. In 1921, enforcement of prohibition was joined with enforcement of the anti-narcotics laws. The anti-saloon activities, however, were not received enthusiastically by the Federal law enforcement establishment, and the Commissioner of Internal Revenue repeatedly tried to have prohibition enforcement transferred to the Department of Justice. The Attorney General just as often refused to accept the responsibility. Finally, in 1925, a brigadier general was appointed to the newly created position of Assistant Secretary of the Treasury with specific responsibility to enforce the Volstead Act.

Successful rum-running and distribution of illegal spirits required a large-scale illegal network. The bootlegger became the "friendly neighborhood supplier" of illicit liquor, and his activities were looked upon with tolerance and gratitude by otherwise law-abiding citizens. Prohibition enforcement agents became the enemy of many of these upright citizens who preferred a drink now and then to rigid enforcement of an increasingly unpopular law. One of the natural consequences was an ever-widening pattern of corruption of law enforcement agencies. The stage was being set for the emergence of organized crime syndicates, which would haunt the United States for many decades.

By 1930, over half of the arrests and prosecutions in the Federal courts alleged violation of the prohibition laws. The burden on the Federal courts and on the character and quality of law enforcement was devastating. President Herbert Hoover was shocked at the results of a study by the National Commission on Law Observance and Enforcement. He recommended to Congress a major reorganization in the Federal court system, consolidation of enforcement agencies, and expansion of Federal correctional facilities. The study commission had been created in 1929 under the chairmanship of George W. Wickersham, a former Attorney General, and had conducted a sweeping investigation of all aspects of law enforcement, with sobering results. The Wickersham Commission concluded that corruption in connection with liquor traffic was more extensive than at any earlier time in history. The Wickersham Commission cited the repeated prosecutions of entire law enforcement structures, including police, prosecuting officials, and administrative agencies.

The members of the commission also pointed out the decline in public confidence in Federal law enforcement. They noted the poor character and shoddy appearance of many prohibition agents, whose work was so sloppy that Federal prosecutors and judges had little confidence in the evidence they presented. The commission reported, furthermore, that trial juries were unwilling to believe testimony from these witnesses. Although there were a large number of prohibition arrests, the conviction rate was extremely low.

The Wickersham Commission also cited studies of local law enforcement which showed that local officials had become increasingly ineffective during the prohibition era. Studies in New York City, for example, had shown that in 1926, out of more than eight thousand felony arrests, only 4 percent had resulted in felony convictions and only 37.7 percent had resulted in any conviction at all, even on lesser charges. The comparable figures in Chicago were 4.9 percent for felony convictions and 19.8 percent for convictions for any type of violation. "Surely something is wrong," commented the commission with marvelous understatement.

A striking example of just what was wrong with law enforcement during the prohibition era was the rise to fame and power of Al Capone, who in time became "Public Enemy No. 1." Capone had started out in Brooklyn as a small-time hoodlum. He went to Chicago in 1919, along with Johnny Torrio, to help "Diamond Jim" Collisimo manage a growing string of brothels. Shortly after the Chicago gangs began to take over illegal distribution of alcohol, Collisimo was shot. Torrio and Capone prospered. Their territory extended into the suburbs south and west of Chicago, and by 1924 they were able to boast that they were in full control of the large suburb of Cicero, where they actually handpicked the mayor and the chief of police. By now there were huge profits coming in from their well-organized traffic in prostitution and liquor and gambling. Employees and bodyguards numbered in the hundreds. Capone acquired a steel-armored, seven-ton limousine. By the time he was twenty-five years old he had reached the peak of power in the underworld.

Eventually, a group of Chicago's leading citizens decided to bring an end to underworld influence in that city. Instead of turning to state and local law enforcement, the "secret six" businessmen went to the United States Attorney for the Northern District of Illinois, George E. Hugh Johnson. With the help of agents of the Bureau of Internal Revenue, Johnson assembled enough evidence over the course of a two-year investigation to obtain a grand-jury indictment filed on June 5, 1931, charging Capone with Federal-income-tax evasion. Capone originally treated the prosecution as something of a joke and entered a plea of guilty on the advice of his counsel, relying on the fact that the longest sentence for income-tax evasion imposed until that time had been eighteen months. When the Federal-district judge indicated that he did not feel bound by any such limitation, Capone withdrew his plea of guilty and went to trial. He was convicted on three felony counts and two misdemeanors, and received a sentence of ten years' imprisonment. Capone emerged from prison a broken man, victim of untreated syphilis. He lived out his last days in seclusion, and quietly died in his bed at the age of forty-eight.

The Capone tax prosecution taught the country an important lesson: the Federal Government could step in where local law enforcement had become corrupt and ineffective.

By the time Franklin D. Roosevelt was inaugurated as President in 1933, the need for a strong role for Federal law enforcement had become acute. Organized crime had expanded its operations into racketeering, kidnapping, and extortion. In addition, the collapse of the stock market and the depression had revealed extensive manipulations in the securities field, thus generating new forms of white-collar crime.

Roosevelt's appointee as Attorney General was Homer Cummings, a lawyer from Stamford, Connecticut. Cummings pushed for a legislative program that contained a Federal law against racketeering, including extortion, violence, coercion, or intimidation. He sought stronger kidnapping laws and other measures to strengthen Federal law enforcement, including Federal statutes against transporting stolen property in interstate commerce; fleeing from prosecution; robbing a bank; assaulting a Federal officer; and importing machine guns. He also organized a national conference on crime and encouraged expanded training of police officers. A new era in Federal law enforcement was dawning.

FEDERAL LAW ENFORCEMENT COMES OF AGE

In late September, 1933, a team of FBI agents surrounded a house in Memphis, Tennessee, the hideout of the most notorious gangster of the day, "Machine Gun" Kelly. The agents identified themselves and ordered Kelly to come out with his hands up. Instead of giving them the shootout they had expected, Kelly meekly walked out the front door, exclaiming, "Don't shoot, G-men! Don't shoot!" His coined phrase stuck, and "G-man" (for "Government-man") soon became a name symbolizing courage and incorruptibility throughout the land.

The reaction of "Machine Gun" Kelly was representative of the awe and respect that had become attached to the Federal law enforcement officers who made up the FBI in the nineteen-thirties and forties. They were tough and creative, and quickly became American folk heroes. The nickname given to them by Kelly became a badge of honor repeated in motion pictures and radio shows for many years. The FBI became the new symbol of Federal law enforcement, and its agents made full use of the new Federal jurisdiction enacted by Congress. As the FBI launched a war against underworld gangs and kidnappers, public confidence soared.

The stature of Federal law enforcement continued to grow during World War II, thanks largely to the FBI's apprehension and conviction of a number of spies and saboteurs. After the war, internal security became big business for the FBI. Probably its most dramatic achievement was the investigation leading to the trial and conviction of Julius and Ethel Rosenberg and their execution as the nation's first atomic spies.

Internal security became a major concern of Federal law enforcement during the nineteen-forties and fifties, and the Southern District of New York was the focus of several dramatic trials, including the prosecution of Alger Hiss, Judith Coplon, and the seventeen leaders of the Communist Party.

Despite national attention on Federal law enforcement in the internal-security field, the morals and integrity of the Department of Justice itself continued to be a source of concern. During the early days of Harry Truman's Administration, the

President appointed Newbold Morris as a special counsel to look into corruption charges. Morris failed to insist on subpoena powers, and when he tried to require Justice Department employees to file financial statements he was summarily dismissed by Attorney General J. Howard McGrath. McGrath was himself dismissed a few hours later, by Truman. Subsequent disclosures revealed extensive abuses in tax enforcement under the direction of Assistant Attorney General T. Lamar Caudle.

The Department of Justice began to expand in earnest after Dwight D. Eisenhower took office. His first Attorney General, Herbert Brownell, Jr., established an Internal Security Division and expanded the Department's activities in prosecuting racketeers and antitrust cases. Brownell's successor, William P. Rogers, established a new Civil Rights Division in 1958 and instituted suits in Southern states to provide equal voting rights. Rogers also established the Organized Crime and Racketeering Section. Antitrust enforcement stiffened during the Eisenhower period, when criminal indictments for price-fixing against the officers of the major electrical-equipment manufacturers produced several widely publicized jail terms for corporate executives.

When "Bobby" Kennedy was appointed Attorney General by his brother, President John F. Kennedy, there was a brief public outcry against nepotism. But Robert F. Kennedy quickly demonstrated his talents and tackled the assignment with remarkable energy and dedication. Increasingly, the Department of Justice took on the role of mediator in civil rights disputes. Following the funeral of civil rights leader Medgar Evers, who had been killed from ambush a few days before, a group of black youths assembled on the main street of Jackson, Mississippi, to vent their frustration. John Doar, an attorney in the Civil Rights Division, stood alone in the no-man's-land between a crowd of armed police officers and the group of young blacks, who were armed with rocks, and persuaded the youths to disband. Voting-rights cases filed by the Department of Justice increased. The Department also tackled the job of desegregating interstate-transportaion facilities. School-integration efforts were extended into Georgia, South Carolina, Alabama, and Mississippi. In the fall of 1962, the Federal courts ordered officials of the University of Mississippi to admit James Meredith as the first black student in its history. Governor Ross Barnett refused. Nicholas deB. Katzenbach, Deputy Attorney General of the United States, took personal charge of a group of U. S. Marshals to provide an escort to insure that Meredith was permitted to enter. Before National Guard troops were able to bring the campus under control, two people had died. When police dogs were turned loose against groups of blacks in Birmingham, Alabama, in May, 1963, Assistant Attorney General Burke Marshall brought the leaders of the white community together to listen to the demonstrators' complaints and arranged a truce that led to gradual desegregation of lunch counters. These efforts all led to the passage of the Civil Rights Act of 1964, which outlawed segregation in places of public accommodation, prohibited discrimination in state programs receiving Federal aid, and opened up countless new employment opportunities.

During the administrations of Attorneys General Kennedy, Katzenbach, and Ramsey Clark, a great deal of attention was paid to the causes of crime and to the objectives of law enforcement. The question became a major campaign issue in the presidential election of 1968. Crime and law enforcement emerged as national concerns. Candidate Richard M. Nixon hammered away at the rising crime rate and pledged a program of "law and order." Attorney General Clark was characterized by opponents as "soft on crime." Nixon pledged a hard line in Federal law enforcement.

In the last annual report filed by Attorney General Ramsey Clark, the mission of the Department of Justice was defined as securing equal justice for all; providing leadership in corrections rehabilitation; speaking out for the cause of justice; and providing effective investigation in enforcement of Federal criminal laws. Clark's successor as Attorney General, John N. Mitchell, charted a simpler, more direct course: he pledged an "all-out attack on crime."

2

THE FRONT LINES

Seated at his desk in his spacious corner office in the Department of Justice Building in Washington, D.C., Assistant Attorney General L. Patrick Gray picked up the telephone and buzzed his secretary. "Get me Michael Hess in New York," he snapped. In a few seconds Mr. Hess was on the line. "Mike," growled Gray in his toughest Navy manner, "the people down here are upset. They think we should scrap your order-to-show-cause plan and send in troops to get those anti-war demonstrators out of there—*now*."

Michael D. Hess, the bright and articulate thirty-year-old chief of the Civil Division in the Southern District of New York, grimaced. This was the third time in less than an hour that he had received a call from Assistant Attorney General Gray. Each time Gray had become increasingly forceful in his attempt to persuade the United States Attorney's office to send in helmeted park police with billy clubs to "knock a few heads" and thus bring a quick end to the occupation by Vietnam War veterans of the Statue of Liberty in New York Harbor. Gray dismissed arguments that it was better to go before a judge and obtain a court order. He had no patience with the notion that the demonstrators should be given a chance to show cause before some Federal court why they should not vacate the international landmark. It never occurred to Gray that there was something incongruous about sending Federal officers with truncheons against a handful of war veterans holed up in a world-famous symbol of liberty.

The day had begun in confusion. The early-morning radio news broadcasts had carried the first reports about the group of thirteen veterans who belonged to an organization called "Vietnam Veterans Committee Against the War." The veterans had occupied the historic copper-covered structure on Liberty Island shortly before closing time the previous evening. They had then barricaded the door so it could not be opened by the staff in the morning. The incident had thrown the National Park Service into near-chaos, since it was not equipped to deal with such a confrontation.

When I arrived at the office, I called in the executive staff for an emergency meeting. We discussed various alternatives for dealing with the takeover and, instead of resorting to force, agreed to commence a civil injunction action to compel the veterans to move out under threat of contempt. Only a short while before, another group of Vietnam veterans had staged a sit-in demonstration on the Mall in Washington, and Federal officials there had forcibly dragged them away, causing a number of injuries and creating a particularly bad image of the Government in its repressive actions. In New York, we decided to take the initiative ourselves to gain control of the situation and insure that matters would proceed on a more sensible course.

I telephoned the head of the regional office of the National Park Service and discussed the proposed plan of action with him. The superintendent was obviously relieved that someone was doing something to help him in his hour of trial. Then I put in a call to Harlington Wood, Jr., the capable and decent assistant to the Deputy Attorney General. Mr. Wood also liked the idea and called back a little later to report that the New York office had clearance to go ahead.

That was why L. Patrick Gray was not able to specifically *order* Michael Hess to scrap the due-process approach. Gray's own superior had already told the New York office to proceed with the plan. Nevertheless, a good-sized force of special park police had been rushed from Washington with "riot equipment" and was waiting on the New Jersey side of the harbor for orders to land on the island and physically remove the demonstrators.

The media anticipated possible bloodshed, and several television stations had telephoned the courthouse asking what time "the assault" was going to take place. They wanted to have their camera crews ready. But the lawyers had a different idea. They were determined to avoid injury as well as damage to the statue. They were convinced that if the demonstrators were allowed to make their point they would vacate the premises peaceably.

Gray repeatedly urged Hess to forget the injunction proceeding, but the younger lawyer stood firm. "The order to show cause is already upstairs with the judge," he told Gray. "Yes, I believe we can get it served. The attorney for the veterans' committee has already agreed to accept service. The injunction should be argued tomorrow morning and with any luck we should have an order signed by early afternoon."

The plan went off on schedule. The following morning the judge heard argument from the Government and then from the attorney for the veterans. Everyone had his say. The court then granted the Government's application, signed an order directing the veterans to leave, and, lo and behold, they did, quietly and well-behaved.

No one was hurt. The Statue of Liberty was unscarred. The excursion boats began running again. Groups of visitors were once more wearily making their pilgrimage to climb inside the copper lady. The special park police went back to Washington.

THE UNIQUE ROLE OF THE UNITED STATES ATTORNEY

"The United States Attorney," wrote Justice Sutherland in 1935, "is the representative not of an ordinary party to a controversy, but of a sovereignty whose obligation to govern impartially is as compelling as its obligation to govern at all; and whose interest, therefore, in a criminal prosecution is not that it shall win a case, but that justice shall be done. As such, he is in a peculiar and very definite sense the servant of the law, the twofold aim of which is that guilt shall not escape or innocence suffer. He may prosecute with earnestness and vigor—indeed, he should do so. But, while he may strike hard blows, he is not at liberty to strike foul ones. It is as much his duty to refrain from improper methods calculated to produce a wrongful conviction as it is to use every legitimate means to bring about a just one."

According to this standard, the record of United States Attorneys over the years has been uneven. There have been some extraordinarily able and conscientious United States Attorneys, as well as some extraordinarily incompetent ones. Despite occasional blots on the office, however, the United States Attorney has been a dynamic force in the development of Federal law enforcement. The nature of the office as it exists today contains elements of governmental genius which need to be analyzed, distilled, and preserved.

The position of United States Attorney was created under the Judiciary Act of 1789. The statute provided for the appointment in each Federal district of "a meet person, learned in the law to act as the attorney for the United States." His statutory duties were to "prosecute in each district all delinquents for crimes and offenses cognizable under the authority of the

United States, and all civil actions in which the United States shall be concerned." From the outset United States Attorneys had a unique responsibility as public legal officers: they had both *criminal* and *civil* jurisdiction, as well as a broad discretion as to whether and, if so, how to institute enforcement proceedings.

Most state prosecuting officials are limited to criminal enforcement power and therefore have few options in dealing with antisocial conduct. This is a distinction of largely unrealized significance. The civil jurisdiction of the Federal prosecutor is one of the great potential tools for achieving social goals. Unfortunately, national law enforcement leadership, lacking imagination and initiative, has failed to make full use of this special combination of legal tools.

For seventy years, United States Attorneys operated in splendid isolation. Although the Judiciary Act of 1789 established an office of Attorney General of the United States, that official had limited powers and absolutely no voice in how the United States Attorneys performed their responsibilities. Each was a king in his own domain, appointed by the President of the United States and directly answerable to him alone. With the advent of the Civil War, however, it became apparent that some degree of centralized supervision over U. S. Attorneys and U. S. Marshals was necessary to avoid total chaos whenever each district went its separate way. Congress enacted a statute in 1861 giving the Attorney General "superintendence and direction" of those officials, although there was no significant exercise of that power for several years. Finally, in 1896, Congress empowered the Attorney General to appoint Assistant U. S. Attorneys. At last he had a direct say in how the local offices were staffed and run.

In 1906 Congress authorized the Attorney General to participate directly in the conduct of legal proceedings, including grand jury investigations, in the various U. S. district courts. This was the final step in transferring the final word in the conduct of government cases from the United States Attorney to the Attorney General. Congressional action in 1966 provided that each United States Attorney would be appointed for a term of four years.

Except where Congress has expressly authorized attorneys for specialized agencies to appear in Federal court (for example, attorneys for the SEC handle all civil cases involving the securities laws) the United States Attorney acts as the attorney for the Government in all proceedings in which the Federal Government is a party. On the civil side, he advocates the position of the Government in litigated matters, subject, of course, to the instructions he receives from his "client," the particular agency that is directly involved. Frequently, client agencies will take doctrinaire bureaucratic positions on questions raised in civil litigation, and the United States Attorney then plays an especially important role in taking direct responsibility for assuring that the position he ultimately advances on behalf of the Government is a fair and just one, and not merely the narrow view of some administrative official.

On the criminal side, the United States Attorney is vested with extraordinarily broad discretion. Although he is subject to the direction of the Attorney General, the Attorney General is not in a position to review the facts and various considerations that go into most cases, and the job therefore falls to the United States Attorney. His decision whether to prosecute is not subject to review by any court, in keeping with the Constitutional separation of powers. Even when a grand jury returns an indictment, a United States Attorney may refuse to sign the document, thereby rendering it null. And after an indictment has been filed, the United States Attorney has full power to ask the court to dismiss the charges at any time before trial, subject, of course, to his obtaining prior approval from the Department of Justice in most cases.

The discretionary power to decide whether to prosecute is awesome. If the United States Attorney abuses this power, the only available remedy is removal. Although the Attorney General can overrule a United States Attorney and direct the institution or discontinuance of a criminal proceeding, this type of action runs risks in the arena of public opinion.

The Department of Justice has built up specialized groups of trial attorneys who are sent into the field to present complex cases to grand juries and to handle the subsequent proceedings in districts where the staff of the United States Attorney's office is not sufficiently large or experienced. A good U.S. Attorney's office, however, is usually much better equipped to handle a complex criminal prosecution than the young trial attorneys from the Department of Justice, who travel around the country primarily because they are looking for courtroom experience.

THE NATURE OF THE JOB

What does the United States Attorney do?

He is administrator, troubleshooter, enforcement planner, interviewer, litigator, statesman, paper-pusher, back-slapper, adviser, writer, researcher, negotiator, interviewee, and a dozen other things as well. Here is a typical day in the Southern District of New York. Bear in mind that this activity occurs at a rapid-fire pace, usually with a string of telephone calls interrupting; Assistants, job applicants, or other visitors waiting; and deadlines looming.

8:29 A.M.   Breakfast meeting in uptown hotel with Associate Director of the FBI and members of his staff to discuss improved coordination of investigations.

9:52 A.M.   Arrive in office. Quick look at morning mail and telephone messages.

10:04 A.M.   Telephone calls from reporters in pressroom, who have learned from U. S. Marshal's office that James Hoffa is appearing before grand jury. Place call to press officer at Department of Justice in Washington to warn him not to comment if he receives inquiries.

10:22 A.M. Telephone call to Federal bank examiner's office to request accounting help on international financial investigation.

10:36 A.M. Conference with chief of Criminal Division on problem in pending trial.

10:49 A.M. Telephone conference with New York City official to set up joint conference on environmental enforcement problems.

11:17 A.M. Conference with chief of Official Corruption Unit on progress of investigation into Government AID program and possible corruption of officials.

11:43 A.M. Meeting with representatives of GSA on space allocations in proposed new office building.

12:35 P.M. Luncheon conference in library with Executive Assistant and Chiefs of Criminal and Civil Divisions to discuss progress of New York City suit challenging constitutionality of Federal welfare laws; also review of proposals to relieve overcrowding at Federal detention headquarters.

2:13 P.M. Interview of applicant for position as research assistant.

2:46 P.M. Telephone conference with Assistant Attorney General in charge of Criminal Division on problems caused by press leak on Hoffa appearance before grand jury; discussion of status of investigation into police corruption; possibility of establishing special unit to investigate policy-gambling operations at upper echelon.

3:18 P.M. Telephone conference with counsel to New York City Knapp Commission concerning financial assistance from the Law Enforcement Assistance Administration to permit continuation of investigation into local police corruption.

3:34 P.M. To NYC Bar Association for meeting of special committee on current legal problems, including criminal sentencing disparities.

6:28 P.M.   To Fordham Law School to deliver speech at annual dinner of *Fordham Law Review* on the quality of justice in the courts.

10:16 P.M.   Home to bed.

Most days are like this, some with intense pressure because of an emergency problem; some broken up with a parade of visits by members of the staff, or scores of telephone calls; some involving trips to Washington; others devoted to court appearances while the paperwork piles up.

Although a United States Attorney is frequently selected because of his trial experience, his job tends to involve more administration than litigation. Hence, an energetic United States Attorney only occasionally finds the opportunity to try an important case.

The first priority in the United States Attorney's job is keeping track of all cases in which the Government is a party. An office of any size is likely to have at least several hundred cases pending at any one time, sometimes several thousand.

The United States Attorney must maintain proper relations with the Federal judges in his district. This is a delicate balancing act, for the United States Attorney is a litigant who may not engage in *ex parte,* or private, communication with the judge. He is also a public official and officer of the court who must answer for the quality of the presentations made by his staff. At times, judges are overbearing in their treatment of younger Assistants. At other times, judges make serious errors that prejudice the rights of defendants or the Government. The U. S. Attorney must deal with these kinds of problems in a diplomatic and proper way.

Relations with the various divisions in the Department of Justice are also an important part of the job. Every public official feels that his own work is the most important. The U. S. Attorney regularly receives complaints about the failure of his office to provide current information about the status of cases.

There are also always problems in obtaining prior authorization for travel expenses and expert-witness fees. And there are many cases, such as election cases, civil rights matters, and internal security matters, where it is necessary to secure the Justice Department's prior approval of investigations or prosecutions. The Department itself can be extremely slow in answering mail, and frequently reacts in a bureaucratic, negative way to simple requests, so that weeks of patient negotiation are necessary before a sensible course of action can be implemented. All of these administrative matters mean letters, memos, telephone calls, and frequent visits to Washington. Sometimes the matters are truly significant; more often they are picayune.

Dealing with other public agencies also takes a surprising amount of time. Frequently the jurisdictions of neighboring United States Attorneys and local district attorneys overlap. Petty jealousies invariably crop up, particularly if a case is likely to end up in the news media. A tug-of-war often ensues, requiring telephone negotiations or conferences. Sometimes interagency relations deteriorate badly because of an unreasonable or defiant attitude on the part of some staff members. These problems can produce insurmountable obstacles later, when cooperation is essential to effective law enforcement. These same problems may arise with client agencies whose cases are being handled by the office in court. Sometimes an agency will drag its feet providing required factual material. Other times the agency counsel will disagree with the legal position that the Assistant U. S. Attorney plans to assert. These situations all require mediation and take time.

Problems can also arise in dealings with Federal investigative agencies, who are notorious prima donnas when it comes to their prerogatives. Many investigators assume a professional aloofness when an Assistant U. S. Attorney ventures to suggest a course of investigation. "We'll make the investigative decisions," is the usual response. "You handle the legal questions." This type of approach, of course, results in frequent standoffs in which cases are not properly prepared because the agency will not assign personnel to do the work. Investigative agencies, in turn, have good grounds for annoyance when cases they regard as important do not receive priority attention from the U. S. Attorney's office. All of these problems frequently take substantial time and considerable nervous energy.

Serving the press is another time-consuming part of the U. S. Attorney's job. Reporters are constantly seeking stories. Recognition by the media is one of the compensations for a United States Attorney and his staff, and the temptation to leak information or overstate the importance of a case in order to break into print can present serious problems. There is also the need for maintaining centralized control in order to prevent improper leaks. Possibly as much as 20 percent of the day is taken up with press problems of one type or another. These are matters the U. S. Attorney must deal with himself. Congress has provided no public-information officers.

Personnel matters also take a substantial amount of a United States Attorney's time. The recruitment of a capable staff should be uppermost in his mind. If the office is a large one, there is generally a regular turnover in Assistants, since most of them serve for only about three years, to gain courtroom experience. This means that interviews of possible replacements are going on constantly. Even with a full staff, the problems of promotions, pay raises, and special awards for outstanding service all create secondary morale problems and require constant attention.

The professional standards of the office itself also demand attention. Training young Assistants and attending to the standards of professional performance are part of the responsibility of the United States Attorney. If he can, he should visit courtrooms regularly to see the Assistants at work. He should arrange for guest speakers and for sessions to review trial techniques and professional standards.

We have not yet even mentioned the substantive side of the

U. S. Attorney's job. This includes reviewing briefs on appeal and the positions taken in important cases in the office. Frequently, it is necessary to confer about what defenses to assert in a civil case, or what position to argue on a motion. Criminal cases also consume a substantial amount of time, from the initial investigative decisions and progress reports through the decisions on whether to prosecute and on what grounds. Problems of preparing cases for trial often require participation by the United States Attorney, who must on occasion negotiate travel authorization to enable an Assistant to interview a witness, or arrange for some high official to appear at trial.

In the smaller United States Attorneys' offices, the U. S. Attorney himself will not only perform these functions but will handle much of the courtroom work, too. In the larger metropolitan districts, he is likely to spend most of his time on the telephone behind his desk, or in conference. He is also frequently called upon to make speeches and to receive delegations of high-school students or foreign visitors. As he is the chief legal officer in the district, and often the highest-ranking presidential appointee, almost everyone, it seems, has some problem to bring to the personal attention of the United States Attorney.

CRIMINAL PROSECUTIONS

Criminal cases come into the United States Attorney's office from a number of sources. Most grow out of the arrest of individual violators by Federal investigative agencies. Such cases include postal theft, bank robbery, automobile theft, theft of property from interstate shipments. The appropriate investigative agency will usually bring the defendant directly to the courthouse—the FBI, Secret Service, Post Office Inspectors, or other investigative body. An Assistant U. S. Attorney then prepares a written complaint and takes the defendant before the magistrate for arraignment, fixing of bail, and assignment of counsel.

A second group of cases consists of those developed initially by investigative agencies and then referred to the United States Attorney with a "prosecutive memorandum" outlining the facts in considerable detail. Typical prosecutions of this sort include income-tax fraud and securities fraud.

The third major source of prosecutions consists of cases initiated within the United States Attorney's office itself, sometimes in cooperation with one of the Federal investigative agencies. These cases are often the most important Federal criminal cases, and their success depends largely on the staff's strength and experience. Notable recent examples of this type of prosecution include the indictment of former Vice-President Spiro Agnew by the U. S. Attorney's office under George Beall, in Baltimore; prosecution of public officials and organized-crime figures by the U. S. Attorney's office under Herbert Stern and Frederick Lacey, in Newark; and conviction of state and local public officials in Illinois by the U. S. Attorney's office under James Thompson, in Chicago. The primary investigative tool in these cases is the Federal grand jury.

The decision to institute a prosecution is the hardest one a United States Attorney must make, because the consequences are so devastating to all concerned. It is not unusual for the prosecutor to decline prosecution in two cases out of every three. By contrast, local district attorneys usually have prosecutive decisions made for them by the police officers or complaining witnesses who originally instituted the proceedings. As a result, their area of discretion is limited. Once a violation of law has been clearly established, the prosecutive decision generally involves such questions as whether the prosecution will serve any useful purpose either in salvaging the defendant or in serving as a deterrent to others. Part of the decision process, of course, is the need for evenhandedness and fair play. Frequently a case will arise where a young person has been arrested for committing a Federal offense and it is apparent that the jolt of the arrest alone is enough to insure that the defendant will never violate the law again. Such a consideration has become increasingly institutionalized in programs for deferred prosecution, where structured supervision of the defendant is substituted for the traditional criminal court proceeding.

In the typical prosecution of a Federal offense the various steps generally fall into a fairly clear pattern. Each case is assigned to an Assistant United States Attorney, who has full responsibility for handling all stages of the proceeding. His first job is to review the case to determine whether there are any extraordinary problems, such as the impending expiration of the statute of limitations, which require immediate attention. If the defendant is to be arraigned, the Assistant must prepare the necessary papers and reach a decision as to the amount of bail to be requested. Where the defendant has committed a serious violation and has no roots or ties that will assure his appearance for trial, substantial bail is likely, and accordingly the case must receive priority attention. Where a defendant is held in jail, the rule in a district like the Southern District of New York is that the case should be presented to the grand jury for indictment within ten days of arrest. In non-jail cases, twenty days is the usual time. Where speedy trial rules are in effect, the routine Federal criminal case is usually brought to trial within sixty days; the more complicated case within a few months, with six months the maximum. After the filing of the indictment, the Assistant handles the pretrial stages of the case, including the initial pleading on the indictment, at which time bail is reviewed, and whatever motions may be made, usually seeking more details about the nature of the offense. Then, subject to scheduling of the trial by the judge, he arranges for the appearance of witnesses and prepares the case for trial; this includes a fair amount of paper work—writing up legal briefs and requests for legal instructions to the jury. He will then go to court on the appointed day, pick the jury, try the case, and handle any appeal.

The most important function performed by any Assistant

United States Attorney is the exercise of his own independent professional judgment as to the merits of the case and the propriety of prosecution. In the run-of-the-mill Federal violation, the initial investigative work is done completely by experienced special agents, who report orally or in writing the results of their work. A conscientious Assistant will review this investigation independently, including interviewing the principal witnesses, before making a final decision to proceed with prosecution.

Plea bargaining is not as commonplace in the Federal courts as in the state courts. This is partly because the calendar pressures in the Federal courts are less and partly because Federal criminal statutes are usually not divided into different grades of offense to permit negotiation. It is not uncommon, however, for a defense counsel to seek a commitment from an Assistant to dismiss remaining charges if a defendant pleads guilty to one or more counts in a multi-count indictment. The usual rule of thumb here is for the Assistant to be satisfied that there is ample latitude for the court to impose a meaningful sentence if it wishes to. Since most Federal felonies carry a five-year maximum, a plea to one or two counts is usually sufficient to accommodate any typical Federal sentence. In many Federal districts, the U. S. Attorney follows the practice of not making any sentence recommendation to the court, thereby avoiding the most troublesome feature of plea bargaining. The matter of sentence is left entirely to the discretion of the district judge.

PATTERN OF FEDERAL CRIMINAL PROSECUTIONS

Each month the Criminal Division of the Department of Justice issues a summary of recent cases instituted by various U. S. Attorneys' offices around the country. The original selection of the cases is made by the respective United States Attorneys and therefore reflects their evaluation of what are the most important cases in their districts. These summaries, as a result, provide an excellent overview of how Federal criminal law enforcement is currently being implemented throughout the country. It shows the strengths of the present system, and also many of its weaknesses.

Following is a summary of the type of criminal prosecution regarded as significant enough to be reported in a monthly report issued by the Department in 1972:

Alabama, Middle District. Illegal gambling.

Alabama, Southern District. Narcotics; illegal "numbers" operations; income-tax fraud.

Arkansas, Eastern District. Kidnapping of taxi driver; illegal pinball machines.

Arkansas, Western District. Bank kickback scheme; preparation of fraudulent tax returns; perjury.

California, Central District. Tax fraud; mailing of threatening letter; marijuana smuggling.

California, Northern District. Demonstrators indicted for assault; narcotics violation.

California, Southern District. Narcotics; tax fraud.

Delaware. Perjury during gambling investigation.

Florida, Southern District. Tax evasion; union embezzlement; selling stolen antique cars.

Georgia. Tax fraud; fraudulent Medicare claims; bank fraud.

Illinois, Northern District. Extortion.

Iowa. Water-pollution violations.

Kentucky, Eastern District. Misapplication of bank funds.

Maine. Bankruptcy fraud.

Maryland. Union embezzlement.

Michigan. Selling cocaine.

Minnesota. Filing forged documents.

Mississippi, Northern District. Refusal to pay taxes.

New Hampshire. Pension-plan fraud.

New Jersey. Accident-fraud scheme; illegal rebates; reducing-pill fraud; smuggling hashish; stolen-car conspiracy; illegal use of electronic device.

New York, Southern District. Securities fraud; bribing
mutual-fund manager; tax evasion; tax frauds; consumer-
fraud; false financial statements.

North Carolina, Eastern District. Narcotics; shipping
poisoned chicken-treatment compound.

Ohio, Northern District. Attempted murder of new-
born child aboard aircraft; illegal "numbers" operation.

Ohio, Southern District. Attempted extortion.

Pennsylvania, Middle District. Fraudulent applications
for flood relief; extortion.

Pennsylvania, Western District. Illegal diversion of
drugs.

Rhode Island. Union kickback scheme.

Texas, Northern District. Smuggling marijuana; illegal wiretapping.

Texas, Southern District. Tax frauds; failure to file tax
returns; smuggling marijuana; illegal transportation of
explosives; firebomb scheme; bank fraud.

Washington, Eastern District. Narcotics violations.

Altogether, this summary of cases identifies several important
affirmative aspects of current Federal law enforcement: (1) heavy
emphasis on narcotics prosecutions, an area where the Federal
Government's role is critical to achieving any meaningful control of the heroin black market; (2) attention to protecting
union funds against dishonest officials; (3) increasingly vigorous
prosecution of white-collar criminals, including bank officers,
lawyers, and securities-law violators; and (4) prosecution of
those engaged in corruption of public officials at all levels of
government. These are all areas of enforcement where the Federal Government can and should consistently make a positive
contribution.

However, a negative side of current Federal law enforcement practices also shows up in the summary of cases. One of
the most obvious problems is the lack of a coherent national enforcement policy. It is evident that the resources of many United
States Attorneys' offices and Federal courts are being squan-
dered on local gambling prosecutions with little effect. In a

period of extensive *legalized* gambling, it is hard to justify the use of the resources of Federal law enforcement against an activity that is obviously so widely accepted by the community. New thinking about the Federal Government's role in this area is long overdue.

The complete monthly report from which this summary is taken also raises serious questions about the excessive use of criminal sanctions. Witness the indictment of a manufacturer of swimming pools for technical violations of the Truth-in-Lending Act; the prosecution of an alcoholic who participated in a ludicrous attempt to rob a bank in New Jersey which was so ineffective that he was apprehended by two female employees; and the filing of criminal charges for violations of Federal regulations relating to tobacco allotments, interstate shipment of chemical compounds, and violations of the Migratory Bird Act. These are proper subjects for civil or administrative attention, not for all the trappings of Constitutional due process in the United States courts.

Another obvious misuse of Federal law enforcement resources is in dealing with political protest. Persons engaged in "tax rebellions" as a form of war protest should be dealt with patiently and through administrative channels. Obviously the nation must collect its revenues, but criminal prosecutions against people because of their political views is not the function of a system of equal justice. The same is true of the case of the young man who sent his draft card back to his local draft board, refused to fill out forms for reissuance of another card, and was thereupon sentenced to one year in prison. Plainly, evenhanded law enforcement requires a policy of prosecuting those who refuse to enter military service in wartime when their turn comes. At the same time, criminal prosecution is plainly inappropriate for those who mail back a draft card as an act of war protest. Such heavy-handedness, in addition to everything else, helps to generate distrust of the administration of justice and disrespect for the law.

On a related question, the criminal prosecution of persons who send threatening letters through the mail also seems questionable, unless the letters themselves really inflict harm. What usually is needed is treatment for a personality disorder.

The monthly case summary also graphically demonstrates irrational differences in sentencing practices between the various Federal districts. Sometimes, too, between individual judges in the same district. In the Eastern District of North Carolina, for example, two defendants were convicted of assisting in the preparation of false income-tax returns and received only nominal *fines,* while a third defendant convicted for exactly the same offense—but sentenced by a different judge—was sent to prison for *three years.*

In the Southern District of Mississippi, two "respectable" members of the community who pleaded no contest to charges of willful failure to file income-tax returns—a doctor and a lawyer—were *fined* three thousand and two thousand dollars, respectively, while a conscientious objector who failed to report for civilian work to which he had been assigned was sentenced to *prison* for *five years.*

In the Western District of North Carolina, a former bank vice-president was convicted for embezzling over fifty thousand dollars from his bank and was *fined* only six thousand dollars. At about the same time, in the Western District of Oklahoma, an individual was convicted for burglarizing a mail truck and stealing a hundred welfare checks (collectively worth substantially less than fifty thousand dollars) and was sent to *prison* for *five years.*

A former county attorney, convicted in the Western District of North Carolina of stealing funds from an estate, was *fined* two thousand dollars. In the same month a female employee was sent to *prison* for *four years* for embezzlement from a credit union in the Southern District of Texas.

Although there are many creditable features of current Federal law enforcement, there are also many that need changing.

3

A LESS-THAN-HALLOWED PLACE

To most observers, Jack Hushen was just a very lucky young man. After working as a reporter for a Midwestern newspaper, he had been handpicked by Attorney General John N. Mitchell to become Director of Public Information for the U. S. Department of Justice. After Mitchell resigned, Hushen stayed on in the post under Mitchell's successor, Richard G. Kleindienst. After Kleindienst and his boss, Richard Nixon, resigned, Hushen moved over to the White House as Deputy Press Secretary to President Ford. That kind of track record shows a remarkable adaptability to new loyalties, and Hushen won a reputation in the Department for ruthlessness and ambition which fit his role perfectly.

On April 11, 1973, Hushen dispatched the following teletype message to the ninety-three Attorneys' offices around the country.

FM JOHN W. HUSHEN DIRECTOR OF PUBLIC INFORMATION
DOJ WASHDC TO ALL U S ATTORNEYS
SUBJECT WATERGATE
    AT THE WESTERN REGIONAL MEETING OF UNITED

STATES ATTORNEYS IN LATE MARCH, ATTORNEY GEN-
ERAL KLEINDIENST DISCUSSED THE WATERGATE INVESTI-
GATION AND SUBSEQUENT TRIAL IN HIS INFORMAL
REMARKS.
ONE OF THE POINTS HE STRESSED WAS THE EXHAUS-
TIVE NATURE OF THE INVESTIGATION, INCLUDING
THE HUGE NUMBER OF LEADS CHECKED OUT AND
WITNESSES INTERVIEWED. HE ENCOURAGED THE U S
ATTORNEYS ATTENDING THE CONFERENCE (AND ALL
OTHERS) TO NOT HESITATE TO SPEAK OUT ABOUT WHAT
HE TERMS "THE MOST THOROUGH, COMPLETE INVESTI-
GATION BY THE FBI SINCE THE ASSASSINATION OF
PRESIDENT KENNEDY." OUT OF THIS INVESTIGATION
GREW THE EVIDENCE TO INDICT AND CONVICT SEVEN
PERSONS, HE SAID. "WE CHARGED ALL THOSE AGAINST
WHOM EVIDENCE OF ILLEGAL ACTIVITY COULD BE
ESTABLISHED."
TO SUPPLEMENT MR. KLEINDIENST'S REMARKS, I AM
SENDING YOU THE CURRENT STATISTICS ON THE SIZE
OF THE INVESTIGATION AND GRAND JURY ACTIVITY
GROWING OUT OF THE BREAK IN AND BUGGING AT THE
DEMOCRATIC NATIONAL COMMITTEE HEADQUARTERS:

PERSONS INTERVIEWED:	2,347
LEADS CHECKED OUT:	2,698
FBI AGENTS INVOLVED:	343
FIELD OFFICES INVOLVED	56 of 59
AGENT MAN HOURS:	22,403
PAGES OF INVESTIGATIVE REPORTS:	5,500
WITNESSES BEFORE GRAND JURY:	50
DAYS OF TESTIMONY:	44
NUMBER OF PERSONS INDICTED:	7
NUMBER OF PERSONS CONVICTED:	7

I HOPE THIS INFORMATION WILL BE OF USE TO YOU IN
ANY PUBLIC COMMENTS AND SPEECHES YOU MAY BE
CALLED ON TO MAKE.

Four days later, Attorney General Kleindienst met with
Henry E. Petersen, Assistant Attorney General in charge of the
Criminal Division, the United States Attorney for the District
of Columbia, and the Assistant U. S. Attorney who had been
in charge of the Watergate grand jury investigation. When the
meeting ended, Kleindienst immediately withdrew from any
further participation in the Watergate investigation. Two

weeks later he submitted his resignation as Attorney General of the United States, stating that he had learned that "persons with whom I had had close personal and professional associations could be involved in conduct violative of the laws of the United States."

The Attorney General's resignation was accepted by President Nixon on April 30, 1973, the same day he also accepted the resignations of his two top White House aides, H. R. Haldeman and John D. Ehrlichman. The President also announced that he had requested and accepted the resignation of John W. Dean III from his position as White House Counsel. Ironically, the date of the President's announcement was the eve of the nation's observance of Law Day.

One year later, Mr. Kleindienst entered a plea of guilty in the District Court of the United States for the District of Columbia to a criminal-information charge that he had failed to answer accurately and fully questions put to him by a Senate committee during the course of his own confirmation hearings to become Attorney General.

The personal culpability of Mr. Kleindienst will long be debated. Was he simply being used by the White House during the cover-up when he insisted that the Watergate affair had been thoroughly investigated? Was he just being loyal in failing to tell the Judiciary Committee that President Nixon had personally directed him to drop the appeal in the ITT antitrust proceeding? Those who know Richard Kleindienst are inclined to give him the benefit of the doubt. He is bright and personable, a personification of the American dream. The son of a brakeman on the Santa Fe Railroad, Kleindienst graduated Phi Beta Kappa from Harvard and then from Harvard Law School. As a youngster he went to school with Navajo Indians in Arizona, became fluent in their language, and was elected class president. His political activities in Arizona carried him to the state legislature, a 1964 race for Governor, campaign work for Senator Barry Goldwater, and then to the post of National Director of Field Operations for the Nixon campaign in 1968. John Mitchell chose him as his Deputy Attorney General, and when Mitchell stepped down, Kleindienst took over his friend's and former boss's job. His discovery that he might have to prosecute Mitchell after being closeted with the Watergate prosecutors on April 15 led to his resignation. There has been no suggestion that Mr. Kleindienst personally aided in the cover-up operations, but his public-relations efforts as Attorney General certainly served to mislead the American people as to the true facts, of which he later claimed he was unaware.

But the key question is this: how is it possible for the nation's chief law enforcement officer to be so uninformed about an investigation of major national importance conducted on such a large scale by his very own agency?

The ITT matter was seamy and perplexing. There was an ironic twist in the way the whole Kleindienst testimony came about. Confirmation hearings on his nomination to become Attorney General had apparently been concluded in the spring of 1972, when columnist Jack Anderson published the text of a memorandum written by Dita D. Beard, a lobbyist for ITT. The Beard memo, addressed to the company executive in charge of ITT's Washington office, indicated that ITT's commitment to contribute $400,000 toward the Republican national convention in San Diego had aided negotiations to settle a sensitive merger case with the Justice Department. As soon as the Beard memo surfaced in the Anderson column, Mr. Kleindienst demanded that the confirmation hearings be reopened so that he could remove any cloud from his nomination. It was during the reopened hearings that Mr. Kleindienst falsely testified concerning instructions he had received from President Nixon to drop the ITT appeal.

In 1969 the Justice Department had instituted three antitrust proceedings against ITT to force the corporate giant to divest itself of a number of its member companies. After a series of negotiations with the Assistant Attorney General in charge of the Antitrust Division, ITT agreed, on July 31, 1971, to let go of all of the companies except one, the Hartford Fire Insurance Company. The Beard memo suggested that retention of the insurance company had been accomplished because of ITT's commitment to help with the cost of the upcoming Republican convention.

During the Kleindienst confirmation hearings, former Attorney General Mitchell testified that he had disqualified himself from participating in the ITT matter because his former law firm had represented an ITT subsidiary. This left Mr. Kleindienst in charge, along with Richard McLaren, the Assistant Attorney General in charge of the Antitrust Division. Mitchell said that he had not known anything about the ITT pledge of funds for the Republican convention until he read about it in the newspapers long after the settlement. Mitchell conceded that he had had a meeting with the head of ITT while the antitrust cases were pending, but claimed they discussed only "overall antitrust policy of the Department" and not specific cases or the taking of any action.

As the Kleindienst-confirmation hearings bogged down over the ITT matter, the White House considered withdrawing his nomination. A memorandum prepared by Special White House Counsel Charles W. Colson for top presidential aide H. R. Haldeman on March 30, 1972, was subsequently turned over to the Ervin Committee investigating the Watergate affair. That memorandum contained a factual summary of what the official documents showed about the ITT matter. They clearly refuted former Attorney General Mitchell's testimony to the committee. The Colson memo referred to a number of documents indicating discussions between Mitchell and others, including the head of the corporation and the President, about the conduct of the ITT matter. There was also a memorandum from the President's Press Secretary to Mr. Haldeman, with a copy to Mr. Mitchell, a full *month* before the ITT settlement, which spelled out the existence of the $400,000 ITT commitment to help with the Republican convention.

Kleindienst was closely questioned by Senators Bayh, Kennedy, and Hart about possible White House influence in the ITT case. In answer to a question by Senator Kennedy, Kleindienst responded, "In the discharge of my responsibilities as the Acting Attorney General in these cases, I was not interfered with by anybody at the White House. I was not importuned, I was not pressured, I was not directed." At the time of his guilty plea, Mr. Kleindienst admitted that he had in fact received a call from John Ehrlichman, telling him that the President had ordered Kleindienst to drop the appeal to the Supreme Court in a preliminary stage of the case; when he had refused to do so, Kleindienst said, the President had personally called and directed him not to appeal the case.

According to White House tapes subsequently turned over to the House Judiciary Committee during impeachment hearings, this is what actually transpired when the President spoke to Kleindienst about the ITT appeal during a telephone conversation on April 19, 1971:

> *Nixon:* I want something clearly understood. . . . The ITT thing—stay the hell out of it. Is that clear? That's an order. . . . Don't file the brief.
>
> *Kleindienst:* Your order is not to file a brief?
>
> *Nixon:* Your—my order is to drop the goddamn thing. Is that clear?
>
> *Kleindienst:* (laughs) Yeah, I understand that.
>
> *Nixon:* Okay.

A conversation with the President of the United States which one would not be likely to forget.

Mr. Kleindienst explained that after the President's phone call he asked Mr. Mitchell to convey to the President his decision to resign, and that shortly thereafter the President retracted the order and the case was in fact appealed. Following this incident, the disputed settlement was entered into. Mr. Kleindienst expressed deep regret over his action. "I was wrong in not being more candid with the committee and I sincerely regret it." He also said that he was entering his plea of guilty —the first conviction of a cabinet member since Albert B. Fall had been found guilty in the Teapot Dome scandal—"out of respect for the criminal justice system of the United States and the indisputable fact that the system must have equal application to all." Despite this reference to equal justice, the district judge before whom Kleindienst appeared praised the former Attorney General for his action and then sent him on his way with no sentence whatsoever. So ended what had once promised to be a brilliant career. And with it, the office of Attorney General of the United States suffered another loss of credibility in the eyes of the public.

A MAN OF "LAW AND ORDER"

The now-familiar story of the break-in at Watergate in June, 1972, and of subsequent efforts to cover up the involvement of White House staff in that illegal activity has a particular significance to the history of the office of Attorney General of the United States. The activities of John N. Mitchell—who came into office as a hard-line "law and order" man—both while he held the office and after his departure, are directly contrary to everything that equal justice and impartial law enforcement should stand for.

During the Senate investigation into the Watergate affair before the Ervin Committee, Mitchell conceded that he had played a substantial role in the Nixon reelection campaign even while he was still running the Department of Justice.

> Q. Did you play an active supervisory role in the campaign before you resigned as Attorney General?

A. What I did was succumb to the President's request to keep an eye on what was going on over there and I had frequent meetings with individuals dealing with matters of policy; also with individuals who would bring other individuals over to introduce them to me and discuss their talents and their qualities with respect to filling certain jobs in that particular area. Yes sir, I did.

Q. You would consider, then, that you did play an active supervisory role before you resigned as Attorney General?

A. If you would change "supervisory" to "consulting," I think I would be much happier.

Q. Did it get beyond the consulting capacity?

A. Well, it might have been in areas where I let them know my opinion quite forcefully and strongly, but I think that would still fit under the role of consultant.

Mitchell had testified directly to the contrary at the time of the Kleindienst confirmation hearings. He had told Senator Kennedy then that he had "no reelection-campaign responsibilities" before he resigned as Attorney General. He attempted to explain away this contradiction in his later testimony, but the fact of his having misled the committee at the time of the earlier confirmation hearings was plain.

In later testimony, Mitchell conceded that campaign strategy meetings had been held in his office at the Department while he was Attorney General, at which proposals were advanced that were clearly in violation of law.

Q. Now, on the 27th of January, 1972, Gordon Liddy presented a plan in your office, in the office of the Attorney General of the United States, and that plan, complete with visual aids, included elaborate charts of electronic surveillance and breaking and entering and prostitution and kidnapping and mugging. Now you have indicated that in hindsight you probably should have thrown him out of the office.

A. Out of the window.

Q. Maybe even out of the window, in hindsight. The life of every American is or to a great degree his liberty, protection of all of his rights, sits in the hands of the Attorney General of the United States, and do you mean to tell me that you sat there through that meeting and, in fact, actually had the same man come back into your office for a second meeting without in any way alerting appropriate authorities in this particular case, the President of the United States?

A. That is exactly what happened, Senator. And, as I say, in hindsight it was a grievous error.

The demeaning of the office of Attorney General for political purposes did not stop there. After he had resigned to become chairman of the President's reelection campaign and after the Watergate break-in had occurred, Mitchell participated in discussions aimed at obstructing the grand jury investigation into the planning and execution of that crime. Those discussions included preparing his campaign aide, Jeb Stuart Magruder, for his grand jury appearance, during which it was agreed he would commit perjury. Mitchell conceded the fact in his Senate testimony.

Q. You also were informed by Magruder that he, Magruder, was prepared to commit perjury when it went before the grand jury in August rather than to reveal what he knew about these matters?

A. That was correct, sir.

Q. Now, did you agree that that was the proper course of action to take?

A. It was a very expedient one, Senator. At that time in the campaign so close to the election, we certainly were not volunteering any information.

Q. Well, did you advise Mr. Magruder that perjury was a felony and he ought not to commit perjury when he proposed to you that he commit perjury?

A. I am sure Mr. Magruder was well aware of it.

Q. Yes. Well, did Mr. Mardian and Mr. LaRue ever talk to you about the Magruder proposal to commit perjury?

A. They were present on an occasion or more in which Mr. Magruder stated what he was going to testify to.

In the midst of the Watergate shock waves another series of incidents involving former Attorney General Mitchell came to light, as a result of an independent grand jury investigation in the Southern District of New York.

On May 10, 1973, a special Federal grand jury in New York filed an indictment charging John Mitchell and Maurice Stans, former Secretary of Commerce and thereafter chairman of the finance committee of the Nixon reelection campaign, with conspiracy to defraud the United States and to obstruct justice. The indictment also charged Mitchell and Stans with committing perjury before the grand jury. The charges centered around a secret contribution of $200,000 paid in cash by Robert L. Vesco to Stans in early April, 1972. At the time, Vesco was the subject of an investigation by the Securities and Exchange Commission and had been attempting unsuccessfully to arrange a conference with William Casey, the chairman of the SEC, in hopes of stopping the investigation. On the very day the cash contribution was turned over to the reelection campaign committee, Vesco's lawyer, Harry Sears, went in to see John Mitchell, who then telephoned the chairman of the SEC and arranged for a meeting that very afternoon for Sears to discuss the Vesco matter. The SEC staff held the line against these and subsequent efforts to influence the investigation, but the attempt by Vesco to buy some assistance from Mitchell was clear. Just the fact that Mitchell had a sufficient interest to telephone Casey about the case could have been enough to tip the scales in Vesco's favor if the SEC staff had not been so firm.

After a lengthy trial before a sequestered jury—from which

had been excluded all persons with more than a minimal knowledge of the Watergate affair, and therefore, by definition, anyone who regularly read the daily newspapers—Mitchell and Stans were acquitted on the legal charges. A key witness in the case was John Dean. Although he had been indicted for his own role in the Watergate cover-up, Dean had not yet been sentenced. Defense counsel cross-examined hard on this point and argued in summation to the jury that Dean was only trying to save his own skin by testifying against Mitchell and Stans and should not be believed. By the time of the subsequent Watergate-conspiracy trial in Washington, in which Dean was also the key witness, he had been sentenced to eighteen months in prison and was already incarcerated. His vulnerability to attack on this issue was eliminated, and, with the additional help of significant corrobation on the Oval Office tapes, the jury had no trouble in returning a guilty verdict.

The Mitchell-Stans prosecution was a complex case with difficult legal problems which would have been hard to win under any circumstances. Newspaper reports of interviews of the jurors after the verdict indicated that most of them had failed to understand the basic issues and that they had been dominated by a single juror, an officer of the First National City Bank, who had developed doubts about the Government's case even before he had heard any evidence. During the trial, the officer arranged for the bank to provide private screenings of motion pictures and other special comforts for his fellow jurors, and himself advanced cash to help pay for meals in expensive restaurants that he himself selected. In time he had become a leader and benefactor in the jurors' eyes. Reportedly the original vote in the jury room was eight to four for conviction, but the bank officer went to work on his fellow jurors until he swung them all around to vote for acquittal.

Notwithstanding the verdict, the evidence at the trial showed that after the $200,000 Vesco payment, Mitchell had initiated steps to prevent disclosure of the secret contribution. As for

Stans, he had talked to Bradford Cook, Casey's successor as chairman of the SEC, discussing with Cook the possibility of changing the complaint ultimately filed against Vesco to eliminate any references which might suggest that Vesco had made payments to the Nixon campaign. The disclosure of high-level government activities surrounding secret campaign cash gifts at a time when a sensitive SEC investigation was under way was alarming.

Mitchell was subsequently convicted for his participation in the Watergate cover-up, and Stans pleaded guilty to five counts of violating Federal election campaign laws.

The indictment of former Attorney General Mitchell in the Vesco case came only ten days after President Nixon's announcement of the resignation of Mitchell's successor as Attorney General, and the departure of the three senior White House aides who had been involved in the Watergate-cover-up scandal. At the time of the indictment, the public was in a state of shock at what appeared to be obstruction of justice at the highest levels of government, particularly in the Department of Justice. In this atmosphere, the action of the special grand jury in New York stood out as a beacon of independence and integrity. Equally impressive had been the dogged work of Assistant United States Attorneys John R. Wing and James W. Rayhill, later aided by John A. Lowe and Kenneth Feinberg, in putting the case together for trial.

On March 1, 1974, the very day trial against former Attorney General Mitchell got under way in New York City, a Federal grand jury in the District of Columbia indicted Mitchell along with former Assistant Attorney General Robert C. Mardian; White House aides Haldeman, Ehrlichman, Colson, and Gordon C. Strachan; and Kenneth W. Parkinson, attorney for the re-election-campaign committee, on charges of conspiracy to obstruct justice in connection with the Watergate break-in. The principal charge in the indictment included a conspiracy to defraud various Federal agencies, including the CIA, FBI, and

Department of Justice. Mitchell was specifically charged with meeting Mardian in Beverly Hills and asking Mardian to relay a request to Attorney General Kleindienst for assistance in obtaining the release of some of those who had been arrested for the Watergate break-in. Mitchell was also charged with meeting Jeb Magruder, along with Mardian, in Mitchell's apartment and suggesting that Magruder destroy documents in his files. The indictment alleged that Mitchell and Mardian later held a meeting with John Dean, at which it was suggested that the CIA be requested to provide secret funds to assist the persons involved in the Watergate break-in. Mitchell was also charged with authorizing payments to E. Howard Hunt, Jr., one of the principal Watergate-break-in defendants, and with asking John Dean to relay an assurance of executive clemency to another Watergate defendant, James W. McCord, Jr.

The District of Columbia Federal indictment also alleged that Mitchell had submitted false statements to agents of the Federal Bureau of Investigation, and had committed perjury before the Federal grand jury and the Ervin Committee.

All in all, it was a sorry litany of activities on the part of a former Attorney General of the United States. On January 1, 1975, the jury returned its verdict of "guilty" against all of the defendants except Kenneth Parkinson. The verdict confirmed that John N. Mitchell had acted in a fashion totally inconsistent with the standards of integrity and impartiality required of the chief legal officer of a great nation.

THE SATURDAY NIGHT MASSACRE

Not all of the Attorneys General in the Nixon Administration were insensitive to their public obligations. There was at least one notable exception: Elliot L. Richardson. Richardson's brief tenure as head of the Department of Justice raised further questions about the relationship between the Department and the White House, and the subservience of the administration of Federal justice to political considerations of the Administration in power.

Elliot Richardson took over from Richard Kleindienst as Attorney General in May, 1973. A former United States Attorney, Mr. Richardson had held several high-level jobs in the Administration—as Secretary of Health, Education, and Welfare, and then as Secretary of Defense—before he was nominated as Attorney General. Against the uproar over the disclosures of the Watergate cover-up, Richardson pledged to appoint an independent Special Prosecutor to conduct the Watergate criminal investigation without outside interference. Richardson's designee as Special Prosecutor was Harvard Law School Professor Archibald Cox, a former Solicitor General of the United States in the Kennedy Administration.[*]

Following his confirmation as Attorney General, Mr. Richardson left the Watergate investigation completely in the hands of Mr. Cox, while he set about trying to rebuild public confidence in the integrity of the Department of Justice. In a ringing address before the House of Delegates of the American Bar Association at its annual meeting in Washington in August, 1973, Attorney General Richardson told the nation's leading association of lawyers that he felt a special responsibility toward the law and toward the integrity of the Department of Justice. Whatever stains that integrity, he said, damages confidence not simply in the Department but in government itself.

> Confidence is not a structure built of stone that can withstand the buffeting winds of accusation and mistrust. It is the expression, rather, of trust itself. It is as fragile as it is precious, as hard to restore as it is easy to destroy. And yet it is obvious that trust is necessary to the very possibility of free self-government.

[*] The staff assembled by the Watergate Special Prosecutor included a number of Assistant U. S. Attorneys from the Southern District of New York: Richard Ben-Veniste; Richard J. Davis; Jay S. Horowitz; Peter F. Rient; Jon A. Sale; Frank M. Tuerkheimer.

Richardson said that in order to counter the suspicion of political influence in the Department of Justice he was not only foreswearing politics for himself but was asking all of his principal colleagues to do the same. He reminded other departmental employees, including the U. S. Attorneys, that they were prohibited from political action under the Hatch Act.

Richardson also announced a departmental order formalizing a procedure for making a written record of every contact with outside parties concerning any matter pending before the Department, including oral communications. One copy of the written memorandum of each contact was to be kept by the employee and the other was to be placed in the case file. This new procedure specifically included inquiries from members of Congress and their staffs, as well as other government officials and private persons not directly involved in the case.

Unfortunately, the exciting change in policy and leadership in the Department of Justice was destined to be short-lived. When President Nixon announced Mr. Kleindienst's resignation and his nomination of Elliot Richardson as the next Attorney General, the President said that Richardson's job would be to assume full responsibility for coordinating the effort to get to the bottom of the Watergate cover-up. Nixon added Richardson would receive "total support" from the President in his efforts. Less than six months later, Attorney General Richardson was being forced by President Nixon to submit his own resignation after he refused to discharge the Special Prosecutor he had selected to "uncover the whole truth" about the Watergate affair. The episode was a confrontation of power of unbelievable proportions, which left the Department of Justice even weaker than before.

Special Prosecutor Archibald Cox had applied to the Federal courts for an order directing the President to turn over tape recordings made in the Executive Office of conversations relating to the Watergate matter and discussions with the various persons who were involved in the investigation. The United States

Court of Appeals for the District of Columbia had ordered the President to surrender the tapes, but the President abruptly announced that he was going to refuse to comply with the order and would not appeal it to the Supreme Court. Instead, he directed the Special Prosecutor to drop the proceeding. Professor Cox said that he would not accept the President's order and that to do so would violate his obligations to the Senate and to the nation. On Saturday, October 20, 1973, the following events occurred in rapid-fire order. Special Prosecutor Cox announced on a televised news conference that he would return to Federal court in defiance of the President's order, to ask for a ruling that the President had failed to comply with the court's order to turn over the tape recordings. Attorney General Richardson was told by the President that the Special Prosecutor would have to be dismissed. Instead, the Attorney General resigned. A White House aide then instructed Deputy Attorney General William Ruckelshaus to carry out the order. When he refused to do so, he was summarily dismissed. Solicitor General Robert H. Bork, a professor from Yale Law School, became Acting Attorney General and was instructed by the White House to fire his colleague from the Harvard Law School. He did so. Simultaneously, the White House issued orders to the FBI to take control of the offices and files of Richardson, Ruckelshaus, and Special Prosecutor Cox and his staff.

The reaction throughout the nation was one of shock and dismay. Perhaps the most surprising and refreshing voice came from the president of the American Bar Association, which ordinarily avoids matters of public controversy. Chesterfield Smith, reminding the public that his predecessor, Robert Meserve, had called for the appointment of an independent prosecutor on behalf of the American Bar Association the preceding spring, spoke out on behalf of the lawyers of the country in protest against the President's actions.

> Now, the President of the United States, by declaring
> an intention, and by taking overt action, to abort the

established processes of justice, has instituted an intolerable assault upon the courts, our first line of defense against tyranny and arbitrary power. The abandonment, by Presidential fiat, of the time-tested procedures to insure the equitable distribution of justice constitutes a clear and present danger of compelling significance.

President Nixon abruptly reversed himself and agreed to turn over the tape recordings to the district court. The whole upheaval had been for naught. The nation had lost an effective Attorney General, his Deputy, and an independent Special Prosecutor—but much more important, it had lost all confidence in the independence and integrity of the administration of Federal justice—for no purpose whatever. The President had only briefly had his will, but in the exercise of naked power had shown how vulnerable the office of Attorney General of the United States is to political direction from the White House, and what the ultimate penalty is when an incumbent will not accommodate himself to such direction.

THE WHITE HOUSE AND THE ATTORNEY GENERAL

When George Washington selected Edmund Randolph as first Attorney General of the United States, his letter of appointment spoke of the high resolve of the President to help achieve proper administration of justice.

New York, September 28, 1789.

Dear Sir: Impressed with a conviction that the due administration of justice is the firmest pillar of good Government, I have considered the first arrangement of the judicial department as essential to the happiness of our Country, and to the stability of its political system; hence the selection of the fittest characters to expound the laws, and dispense justice, has been an invariable object of my anxious concern.

I mean not to flatter when I say, that considerations like these have ruled in the nomination of the Attorney-General of the United States, and, that my private wishes would be highly gratified by your acceptance of the Office. I regarded the office as requiring those talents to conduct its important duties, and that disposition to sacrifice to the public good, which I believe you to possess and entertain; in both instances, I doubt not, the event will justify the conclusion; The appointment I hope, will be accepted, and its functions, I am assured, will be well performed. . . .

George Washington

If every President and every Attorney General had the same outlook as Washington and Randolph, we would have no need for worry. But times have changed, and the concerns of the President no longer include giving much attention to the due administration of justice. The job of the Attorney General has also changed. No longer is he simply a learned gentleman who occasionally advises the President on legal questions or appears in the Supreme Court on behalf of the United States. The President now has his own staff of aides who supervise governmental functions for him. When an Attorney General or some Deputy receives a call from the White House counsel, he may never know whether the call has been instigated at the request of the President or of someone with an ulterior motive.

The functions of the Attorney General today far exceed the ordinary abilities and capacity of just a lawyer, no matter how outstanding or extensive his experience in the courtroom. The Department has become a vast bureaucracy, with a budget of nearly two billion dollars and a staff of almost forty thousand people, only relatively few of whom are members of the legal profession. The staff includes entire agencies, such as the FBI, the Immigration and Naturalization Service, the Bureau of Prisons, and the Drug Enforcement Agency. As if these responsibilities were not enough, the Attorney General is also a major dispenser of patronage, passing on nominees for the Federal courts, U. S. Attorneys' offices, and U. S. Marshals. He also has an important role in granting pardons and in national policy.

Many well-intentioned people argue that the President is entitled to have a say in the enforcement policy of the U. S. Department of Justice. Examples such as Theodore Roosevelt's vigorous antitrust policy and John F. Kennedy's effective civil rights program stand out as positive arguments in favor of that concept. But where does policy end and politics begin? Given the huge scale of operations of both the White House and the Department of Justice, how can one possibly police the interchange between staff members to insure that only Presidential policy is being communicated and not requests for improper political favors channeled through the White House?

The problem is particularly acute when a politician is in office as Attorney General. As we have seen, both John Mitchell and Richard Kleindienst were active in the political affairs of the Administration. This was nothing new. Harry Daugherty had been Warren G. Harding's campaign manager; Homer Cummings had served as Democratic National Committee chairman; Howard McGrath had been campaign manager for Harry S. Truman; Herbert Brownell had been campaign manager for Dwight D. Eisenhower; Robert Kennedy had been campaign manager for his brother.

Is it enough simply to prohibit active politicians from serving as Attorney General? The impossibility of this solution becomes evident the moment one pursues it. Few people in high government positions have not had some political experience in their background, and indeed such experience is an important part of their perspective. Who can judge which men will be willing to compromise impartial justice for political expediency? Many ambitious officeholders will compromise principle for some personal advantage. Political advantage is just one of many motivations.

While the White House argues that it has a legitimate interest in setting antitrust policies, one of Ralph Nader's investigative teams has studied five antitrust proceedings in which the Administration overruled the recommendations of the career staff of the Department of Justice. Every one involved the economic interests of a substantial campaign contributor. Was this "policy making" or was it politics?

It is argued by some that the Department of Justice can be insulated from political interference by the White House if the Senate carefully scrutinizes the credentials of would-be Attorneys General to make sure they will uphold the ideal of equal justice under law. This view, alas, has proven to be naive. The best expert witness on this subject is John Mitchell. After Mitchell conceded before the Ervin Committee that he had engaged in political campaign planning and strategy discussions while he still held office as Attorney General, Senator Ervin reminded him that at the time of his own confirmation hearings he had promised to perform only *legal* duties for the President, and not political ones. Mitchell's blunt response was that he had not been able to "turn down a request" from the White House.

Even with the best of intentions, how can one keep the White House from interfering in the conduct of the Department of Justice? Mitchell abused the office of Attorney General for political purposes. Kleindienst was apparently kept in the dark while White House staff obstructed an investigation conducted in his own department. Richardson was forced to resign because he would not give in to White House interference. A remedy must be found.

4

BUREAUCRACY AT WORK

In the early nineteen-sixties the chief probation officer in Brooklyn came up with a working procedure for keeping young violators off the criminal court rolls and trying to salvage them while there was still a chance. His concept became formalized as the Brooklyn Plan, which was outlined in a departmental bulletin permitting United States Attorneys to defer prosecution in any case where a defendant agreed to report to the probation department for a period of six months and behaved himself during that period. If the defendant successfully completed the period of voluntary probation, the United States Attorney was authorized to drop all charges against him. The only hitch with the Brooklyn Plan was that it was expressly limited to defendants under the age of eighteen. That is an important group, but far from the bulk of defendants who could be salvaged by proper supervision.

On September 29, 1970, I drafted a letter to the Department on behalf of the United States Attorneys for the Southern and Eastern districts of New York and the District of New Jersey—together representing the largest enforcement area in the coun-

81

try. We recommended that the age limit for the Brooklyn Plan be extended to twenty-five, with the proviso that the prosecutor place in the files a statement explaining why the defendant was put on probation. The probation departments in all three districts said that a number of young people could be diverted from becoming repeat violators if they could be immediately placed under probationary supervision. Receipt of the proposal was duly acknowledged by the Department, on October 16, 1970. Two months later, having heard nothing further, I sent a follow-up letter urging quick action on the request to extend the Brooklyn Plan.

With still no word from the Department, another follow-up letter was sent on March 3, 1971.

On May 12, 1971, yet another letter went off to the Criminal Division, this time offering to modify the proposal in order to provide for court approval of deferred prosecution in each case if that would make it more acceptable. Still no word.

On September 27, 1971, a fifth letter went off to the Department asking where things stood. Still nothing.

Then on December 6, 1971, in the opening address to the National Conference on Correction in Williamsburg, Virginia, Attorney General John N. Mitchell announced that the Department of Justice planned to extend the Brooklyn Plan so that it would apply to older defendants. The draft of the revised plan was sent to the Southern District, which responded that it was "a significant advance in the administration of criminal justice." The matter languished.

On March 8, 1972, the three U. S. Attorneys wrote a further letter, again expressing their enthusiastic support for the proposal to extend the Brooklyn Plan. As this book is being written, almost five years after the initial proposal, the Brooklyn Plan still remains unchanged.

As long as the plan is limited to defendants under eighteen years of age, there is no program to provide community supervision for Federal defendants in the age brackets where most violations occur. The delay in implementing the change is not only inexcusable, it is unconscionable. The whole episode is symptomatic of the lack of initiative in the middle echelons of the Department of Justice. It demonstrates clearly one of the reasons why an overhaul is badly needed.

In the meantime, Senator Burdick introduced legislation in Congress to mandate deferred-prosecution programs in the Federal system. By 1974, the bill had passed the Senate and was under consideration in the House. I appeared in Washington and testified in favor of the Burdick bill, citing good experiences with test cases under a VERA Institute experimental program organized by Harold Baer, Jr., when he was Chief of the Criminal Division in our office. The spokesmen for the Department were lukewarm. If they had shown any enthusiasm and initiative, the program would undoubtedly have long since gone into effect, and hundreds, even thousands, of offenders could have been turned into useful citizens.

*   *   *

In June, 1971, the U. S. Attorney's office recovered a small oil painting believed to be an El Greco sketch made in the early seventeenth century. The painting had apparently been stolen from a house in Spain during the Spanish Revolution. Upon the announcement of its recovery, several persons came forward to claim the valuable object.

Assistant U. S. Attorney Taggart D. Adams, who was assigned to the matter, immediately consulted by telephone with the Criminal Division of the Department of Justice, which had jurisdiction because of the theft feature of the case, and also with the chief of the Foreign Litigation Unit in the Civil Division. A few days later, representatives of the Spanish Consulate called on Mr. Adams, and he explained to them that because of the conflicting claims it would probably be necessary to seek court determination of the ownership before returning the painting. Three separate written claims of ownership to the painting were filed with the United States Attorney's office, by three different law firms. Mr. Adams explored several possible legal means of dealing with the problem and finally concluded that an interpleader suit, which puts all of the conflicting claims before the court for resolution, was probably the best course. He asked for advice from the Criminal Division and the Civil Division in Washington, both of which concurred on this plan of action. On July 20, an interpleader complaint was filed with the District Court of the United States for the Southern District of New York asking for determination of the proper ownership of the painting so that it could be turned over to its rightful owner. The court papers also asked the court to make arrangements to place the painting in the custody of the Metropolitan Museum of Art, which had volunteered to accept it, so that it might be properly cared for and made available for public viewing while the dispute was pending. District Judge Charles L. Brient, Jr., filed an opinion specifying procedures for the care and safeguarding of the painting during the suit. He went out of his way to compliment the United States Attorney's office for taking the proper action, and pointed out that if any harm had come to the painting during the protracted delay it would have been inexcusable.

The Criminal Division of the Department of Justice was equally pleased by the U. S. Attorney's action, and an official letter of August 4, 1971, was most complimentary:

> You have enabled us to turn a potentially difficult matter into an opportunity to protect a very valuable object from possible false claimants while concurrently advancing the public's chances to view the painting.

Two months later, however, L. Patrick Gray III, then Assistant Attorney General in charge of the Civil Division of the Department of Justice, dispatched without warning a three-page single-spaced letter to me as United States Attorney for the Southern District of New York protesting the institution of the interpleader suit; he stated forcefully: "The institution of this suit was not authorized in accordance with the instructions in the United States Attorney's Manual."

The letter went on to explain that the Civil Division in Washington had been researching the question of what action should be taken in connection with the painting and had completed its memoranda on the advisability of instituting an interpleader suit on August 3, two weeks after the U. S. Attorney had already filed the action. In the meantime, the attorney assigned to the matter in the Civil Division had been advising the State Department that the division had not yet decided what action to take. Mr. Gray said that he had been surprised to learn some time later that an interpleader suit had already been instituted. The letter sounded as if it were being sent to the representative of an enemy country.

> This is not the type of suit which falls within authority delegated to the United States Attorney under Departmental Memorandum No. 374. See United States Attorney's Manual, Title 3, pages 26, *et seq*. And, as you know, the institution of a suit outside that delegated authority requires prior authorization from this Division. See United States Attorney's Manual, Title 3, page 3.

The final sentence of the letter was saber-rattling:

> Unless I am satisfied that the interests of the United States are best protected by the suit previously filed, it may be necessary to seek a voluntary dismissal of the suit.

The problem obviously was that the staff man in the Civil Division had not kept his superiors informed, with the result that they were embarrassed in dealing with the State Department because they had not known what was going on. I promptly called Gray on the telephone and told him what the facts were, and followed my call with a letter calling Gray's correspondence "a perfect case study of bureaucracy at its worst." The Assistant Attorney General backed off, but it took a long time to reestablish normal working relations between the Civil Division and the Southern District of New York.

* * *

In May, 1973, an Assistant U. S. Attorney telephoned the deputy chief of the Narcotics and Dangerous Drug Section of the Criminal division in Washington. He urgently requested authorization to move an important witness whose life was in danger to another city. The response that came four days later was classic.

> Pursuant to my telephone conversation with Assistant United States Attorney _____ on May 25, 1973, we are holding your request for witness relocation in abeyance pending the receipt of more specific information concerning this matter. We are particularly interested in knowing of any reports or evidence that would corroborate Mr. _____'s claim that he has been shot at, and whether there is any evidence to reflect that such an attack, if it did occur, was in connection with the testimony given by him at the trial of the above case.

How is that as an example of compassion for one's fellow man?

* * *

Keeping track of case statistics and pending matters has provided a field day for petty officials in the Department of Justice, especially since the advent of data computers. The administrative offices of the United States courts and the Department of Justice have set up duplicate reporting systems, using two different computers and two slightly different data-collecting procedures to assemble exactly the same information about pending cases in the U. S. courts. The number of errors that creep into these systems has grown until it has become virtually impossible to make intelligent use of the data. United

States Attorney staffs are required to spend hundreds of hours trying to straighten out the mess, using old-fashioned hand-written entries to correct data errors in both the Department of Justice printouts and the court's compilations. Repeated efforts to persuade the Administrative Office of the Courts and the Administrative Office of the Department of Justice to work out an efficient cooperative data-collecting procedure have been fruitless.

*　　*　　*

These vignettes are only random samples of what can happen to an agency that has grown too large and lacks effective leadership. The Department's top leaders have been subjected to political domination by the White House. The middle-echelon staff lacks initiative and judgment. The huge civil service bureaucracy has become rigid, doctrinaire, and inefficient. It is time for change.

5

THE DECLINE OF THE FBI

U. S. District Judge Fred J. Nichol is normally a patient man. But on a Monday morning in September, 1974, the judge, sitting in the Federal courthouse in St. Paul, launched into a vigorous tongue-lashing of the Chief Assistant U. S. Attorney from South Dakota. Judge Nichol accused him of being more interested in winning a conviction than in achieving justice. The judge then proceeded to dismiss the grand jury's indictment against leaders of the 1973 Indian uprising at Wounded Knee, South Dakota. He thus ended a criminal trial that had lasted eight months. The incident that provoked the judge's ire was the Federal prosecutor's refusal to accept a verdict by an eleven-member jury after the twelfth juror had been incapacitated by a stroke. That juror had reportedly favored conviction, according to a statement made over the previous weekend by the Assistant U. S. Attorney.

Judge Nichol's criticism of the prosecution was not limited to that incident, however. He also said that the Government had not presented the case properly and had made numerous "errors of judgment and errors of negligence." The judge's harshest words, however, were reserved for the FBI.

"It's hard for me to believe," he said, "that the FBI, which I have revered for so long, has stooped so low."

Earlier during the trial the judge had commented that the FBI had "certainly deteriorated." What precipitated this criticism was a series of events involving misconduct by FBI agents totally at odds with professional law enforcement standards. One incident involved the handling of a government informant whose testimony had been shown to be unreliable and apparently untrue. The FBI informant had been housed during the trial in what was described as a "plush resort." He had been paid substantial sums of cash, and had been escorted on tours of drinking establishments. When the witness was charged with raping a young girl he had picked up while under FBI supervision, the charges were quietly dropped. The implication was that this had been accomplished at the FBI's behest.

The most serious FBI derelictions, however, concerned outright deceptions such as withholding documents from the court and altering evidence provided to defense counsel. During the trial, an FBI agent testified that there had been no interception of telephone calls made by Indians during the Wounded Knee siege. The defense then established that the Bureau had installed a party line and that FBI agents had monitored calls made by Indians. The special agent attempted to explain his earlier misleading denials by saying that he did not consider a party line a "wiretap."

What was perceived by Judge Nichol as a deterioration of the FBI has been observed by many people long connected with law enforcement. They have watched with dismay as the once proud and "untouchable" Federal Bureau of Investigation has been stained by political interference, misuse of authority, and administrative rigidity.

THE DIRECTOR

Long before the office opened for business on the morning of March 7, 1972, the telephone had been ringing vigorously in my room at the United States Courthouse in New York. L. Patrick Gray III, who had recently been promoted to Deputy Attorney General of the United States, the second highest position in the Justice Department, told a secretary it was urgent that he speak to me the moment I arrived. Shortly after 9:00 A.M., I returned the call. Mr. Gray's words were clipped and authoritative.

"You have a witness named Mr. ———— scheduled to appear before the grand jury at ten A.M. John Mitchell has told me to arrange to have the witness interviewed outside the office instead." The man he named was a high political figure in New York State politics.

I patiently explained to the Deputy Attorney General that our practice was to interview all witnesses in the courthouse unless they were working under cover or were cooperating witnesses and there were special circumstances that required secrecy. I asked Mr. Gray if he could provide any additional information about the request so that it could be more adequately evaluated. The Deputy Attorney General said that he would call back shortly.

Meanwhile I got in touch with the Assistant U. S. Attorney who was in charge of the investigation and asked to be filled in on the facts. I explained the nature of the request I had received from Gray and asked for any information he might have about what was behind the unusual call from Washington.

Gray called back shortly afterward. "The request to have the witness interviewed outside the office was made to Mr. Mitchell by Governor Rockefeller," Mr. Gray said. "You can call the Governor's office if you want any more information."

I was incensed. "The answer is NO," I replied. "That is not the way we do things in this office. If the witness has a legitimate basis for requesting an adjournment of his appearance, he can make it directly to the Assistant U. S. Attorney through his lawyer, the same as any other witness."

I told Gray that the grand jury investigation related to alleged security law violations, with organized crime overtones. An informant in the case had reported to the Assistant that one of the subjects of the investigation had been bragging that he had a "fix" in Washington. "He may have been right," I commented.

"That is not very Christian," Gray replied.

Needless to say, the witness appeared before the grand jury.*

Less than two months later, L. Patrick Gray III was promoted again. This time he was selected by President Nixon to become Acting Director of the Federal Bureau of Investigation, to replace the recently deceased J. Edgar Hoover.

During his confirmation hearings before the Senate Judiciary Committee, Mr. Gray blurted out, "I came to this town with reputation and integrity and I'm going to take it away, so help me God!" A few weeks later, Gray's nomination was withdrawn. Not long thereafter, Gray admitted he had destroyed potentially incriminating evidence from White House files. Subsequently he resigned from the FBI in disgrace and returned to his law practice in Stonington, Connecticut.

The character and outlook of the Director of the FBI can have a deep and lasting impact on the agency. Mr. Gray's predecessor held the post of Director for fifty years. J. Edgar Hoover's personal views largely shaped the FBI as it still operates today. Much of what he did was excellent; much, however, fell short.

The FBI reached its zenith of popularity during the late nineteen-thirties, when "G-men" engaged in running warfare with a number of notorious gangsters. The shooting of John Dillinger as he left the Biograph Theatre in Chicago, the killing of "Baby Face" Nelson after a highway gun battle, and the capture of "Machine Gun" Kelly in his hideout in Tennessee, all contributed to a public image of FBI men as tough and skillful. Hollywood movies and magazine articles praised

---

* It turned out that the political leader had told the Governor's office that he was being "harassed" by the U. S. Attorney, and then had refused to deliver the votes needed to pass a major tax bill in the state legislature unless the Governor asked the Attorney General to have the subpoena withdrawn.

the Bureau. The agency's activities made front-page copy week after week.

But the Bureau was not without its critics. Once, during budget hearings, a Southern Senator questioned the Director about his personal background and experience in criminal investigations. The Senator implied that the Director was not willing to face the same dangers he was requiring of his men. Hoover decided then that he would show the world that he could make a daring arrest the same as any other FBI man.

Hoover's target was Alvin Karpis, wanted for extortion-kidnapping in St. Paul. Karpis had sent word to Hoover that he intended to kill him, just as "Ma" Barker and her son had been killed by FBI agents during a shoot-out in Florida. When Karpis was finally located, in an apartment house in New Orleans, the Director flew there with a squad of special agents. Hoover closed in on Karpis as he emerged from the building. Hoover reached into the car that Karpis had entered and grabbed him by the shirtfront, barking, "Put the handcuffs on him." None of the agents, however, had remembered to bring handcuffs. One enterprising young man pulled off his necktie and tied the suspect's hands behind his back.

Hoover's exploit in New Orleans was followed by the surrender of Louis (Lepke) Buchalter, a New York labor racketeer. Buchalter headed the most-wanted list, and news commentator Walter Winchell had broadcast an appeal that he give himself up. When Buchalter made contact, Winchell acted as go-between to negotiate the terms of his surrender. On the night of August 24, 1939, Hoover met the mobster under a street lamp and placed him under arrest. Needless to say, Winchell got the exclusive story.

With all of this publicity for himself and his agency, Hoover became a major force in law enforcement and the administration of justice. As a result, his views carried great weight in setting law enforcement policy. In an approved biography of Hoover and the agency entitled *The FBI Story*, Donald Whitehead reported that the FBI Director was particularly outspoken against what he perceived to be abuses in the correction and parole systems. He lashed out against "sob-sister wardens," prisons that were like "country clubs," and "convict-coddling." Whitehead noted protests that the Director's statements were contrary to probation concepts, but commented, "The FBI Director refused to be gagged—and neither President Roosevelt nor Attorney General Cummings ever made the effort." Considering Hoover's prestige, it is not surprising that the corrections system was slow in developing programs of prisoner rehabilitation. No warden relished the idea of being called a sob-sister by the head of the Federal Bureau of Investigation.

NATIONAL SECURITY

Undoubtedly the single most important factor in shaping the FBI was the institution of domestic national-security intelligence-gathering activities with Hoover's enthusiastic participation. National security created a split in the Bureau's work which made it peculiarly susceptible to political interference from the White House. The long-range result was an undermining of the Bureau's integrity and credibility as a law enforcement body.

According to Whitehead's book, the story of intelligence-gathering by the FBI began in the White House on August 24, 1936, when Franklin D. Roosevelt invited Hoover over for an early-morning conference. "Sit down, Edgar," the President said when Hoover arrived. "I called you over because I want you to do a job for me and it must be confidential."

The confidential job was collecting information on the activities of subversive groups. F.D.R. wanted to obtain a broad intelligence picture of Communist and Fascist activities and their effect on the economic and political life of the nation.

There was no statute authorizing the collecting of domestic-intelligence information by the FBI, so the two men came up with an ingenious scheme. Under the Bureau's appropriation act, the agency was required to undertake investigations requested by the Secretary of State. President Roosevelt instructed Cordell Hull, his Secretary of State, to request an investigation by the FBI into subversive activities. The Secretary complied. Thus began, without congressional mandate, the FBI's national security activities. Over the ensuing years these activities became the dominant force in shaping the Bureau's policies and attitudes. During later years other agencies, including the CIA and Secret Service, joined the national security investigative operations.

Director Hoover became the nation's leading spokesman against "foreign" ideologies. As the years passed, Hoover concentrated on the investigation of "radicals," as he called them. This policy drew increasing criticism from civil liberties spokesmen, who feared the possibility of a police state and political persecution of people who held unpopular ideas. Within Hoover's own organization there was criticism of the obsolete thinking that increasingly guided intelligence-gathering operations. In October, 1971, the number-three man in the FBI, William C. Sullivan, was summarily dismissed by the Director because he criticized the Bureau for focusing on nearly defunct organizations such as the Communist Party and the Ku Klux Klan instead of concentrating surveillance on the New Left and militant groups such as the Black Panthers. Hoover ordered the locks changed on Sullivan's office and his name removed from the door overnight. The Director's failure to keep up with the times was used as one justification for the special White House intelligence-gathering operation that spawned the notorious "plumbers unit" to halt leaks of classified information.

There has been praise for the FBI's intelligence-gathering activities, as well as criticism. The praise comes largely from police officials, who are alerted to potential trouble at local demonstrations as a result of information gathered by FBI informants. Such information permits local police departments to have adequate men on hand when they are needed to minimize violence.

The release in March, 1974, of a group of FBI memoranda on its national security activities, which had been sought by newsmen under the Freedom of Information Act, disclosed that the FBI has gone far beyond mere intelligence-gathering in its operations. Bureau documents revealed a concerted campaign of disruption and harassment as part of the counterintelligence operations conducted by the agency. These operations, all begun under J. Edgar Hoover, included, among other things, long-range efforts to prevent the formation of a coalition of black-nationalist groups and attempts by the FBI to block the emergence of any strong individual who might unify the black-militant movement.

In February, 1975, Attorney General Edward H. Levi disclosed that Hoover had also kept secret files in his own private office, including 48 folders on public figures, among them seventeen members of Congress.

The FBI's intelligence operations have sometimes bordered on the ludicrous. In a recent legal proceeding in New Jersey, the Bureau filed court papers admitting that it had opened a "subversive" file on a sixteen-year-old high-school student who had written a letter to the Socialist Workers Party requesting information about its aims and activities. According to the affidavit, the FBI had instituted a mail watch on the national headquarters of the organization, in New York City, and had copied the student's return address from her letter requesting material. A special agent of the FBI then checked the girl's family's credit, her father's employment, and information from the files of the local police department. When the agent interviewed the high-school principal to gain information on the girl's background and interests, he learned that her letter had been sent to the organization as part of a regular school assignment in political science.

HARDENING OF THE ARTERIES

During his later years as Director of the FBI, Hoover drove to work in a fairly ancient armored car. The vehicle required air conditioning for adequate ventilation. The story is told around the Department of Justice that after a while one of the bearings in the air-conditioning unit became worn and started making a rattling sound. The men in charge of maintaining the vehicle replaced the noisy bearing when the Director was out of town. The following day, Director Hoover was picked up at home, and, using the car's radio, called to complain to the garage that his air conditioner was not working.

"Yes it is, sir. We fixed it yesterday," came the response.

"Well, it's not working now. I can't hear it," Hoover snapped. "Get it fixed."

The car went back to the shop that night, and a crew hastily disassembled the air conditioner and substituted the old bearing for the new one. The next day, with the air conditioner rattling away, Hoover called the garage again. "That's fine," he said. "It's working okay now."

The tendency of the Director to become set in his ways affected the Bureau's operating policies. With the passing years, Hoover's rigidity became the agency's rigidity. The effect on the agents was devastating.

In the beginning of his administration, Hoover had made a number of significant contributions to agency policies and practices. The most outstanding was his insistence on professionalism. He established a training school for the agency at Quantico, Virginia. The FBI National Academy consisted of classrooms, dormitories, and many other features of a small college. Every new agent was required to attend the Academy for fourteen weeks of instruction. More senior agents were sent to Quantico for two-week retraining courses, ranging over such topics as criminal procedure, investigative techniques, and the collection, identification, and preservation of evidence. This same professionalism was extended to FBI training courses for local police officers as well.

Besides undergoing professional training, FBI agents were required to comply with carefully prescribed procedures. All steps in any investigation had to be recorded in writing, on a prescribed form, with regular distribution schedules to insure review by supervisory personnel. Careful attention was paid to activities that might be the subject of adverse comment. Whenever a defense lawyer criticized a special agent during a trial, a detailed report had to be sent to headquarters. Supervisors observed their men on the witness stand. Long before the Supreme Court, in the *Miranda* case, required the police to give warnings to defendants of their Constitutional rights, the FBI had initiated and followed the practice of giving such warnings. All agents were carefully selected, trained, and closely watched. During the early Hoover years it was a source of enormous pride to be identified as an FBI agent.

But then things began to change. The regulations themselves began to dominate the work of the agents. The slightest deviation from the rules produced a written reprimand from the Director himself. Frequently an agent who had failed to comply with regulations was transferred to a distant assignment, at great inconvenience to himself and his family. The initiative and esprit de corps that characterized FBI agents in the thirties, forties, and early fifties began to be replaced by a more cautious don't-rock-the-boat attitude. Fearful of criticism, agents learned it was safer not to show initiative or disregard bureaucratic procedures, no matter how petty.

Director Hoover was ever alert to criticize agents who failed to live within the literal letter of the agency's rules. Once a special agent married a female Assistant United States Attorney, whom he had gotten to know during the course of his work. The agent had failed to give thirty days' advance notice to his superiors as required by the agency's regulations. The purpose behind the thirty-day notice was to give the Bureau an opportunity to conduct an investigation of the prospective spouse to insure that she would not bring discredit to the agency or compromise the agent's ability to perform his duties. Since, in this case, the intended bride was herself an employee of the Department of Justice and had received a comprehensive security clearance conducted by the FBI itself only a short while before, any such notice for investigative purposes was clearly superfluous. Nevertheless, Hoover took the trouble to write an official letter of reprimand to the offending agent. "Your explanation has been considered," wrote Hoover; "however, it is apparent that in this instance you failed to discharge your responsibilities as an employee of the FBI, and you were definitely at fault." The letter ended with a warning to the agent that thereafter it would be incumbent upon him "to display a higher regard for rules and regulations so there will be no basis for similar criticism."

In any other context such a letter would have been uproariously funny. But to an FBI agent a written reprimand from the Director is no laughing matter, particularly when it becomes a permanent part of the agent's personnel file. It is no wonder, therefore, that in its later years the FBI had very few agents who showed any initiative. By the early nineteen-seventies, most of the eighty-six hundred agents of the FBI were either younger men seeking a brief period of law enforcement experience or older agents who had learned to live with the system. Most senior agents had so much invested in their pension rights that they could not afford to leave. The great middle group of experienced, knowledgeable special agents had simply disappeared. A few spirited agents remained. But the others who stayed on were "company men," meekly complying with rules and dreading the nit-picking visits by the inspection staff from Washington. The rest had resigned.

The humorless formalism that overtook the FBI in its later

years is demonstrated in the following letter submitted to one United States Attorney. The letter was sent in connection with an investigation of a Vietnam War draft evader who had gone to live in Canada. The agent who had been assigned the job of locating the fugitive interviewed the youngster's mother. The boy's mother advised the agent that she knew where her son lived in Canada but would not disclose his whereabouts. The FBI solemnly informed the U. S. Attorney that the provisions of the harboring statute, which makes it an offense to harbor a fugitive from justice, had been explained to the mother but that she had still refused to furnish any information about her son's location. The letter then ended with this query: "Would you kindly advise this office at your convenience as to whether or not you wish to consider Mrs. ———— for prosecution under the Harboring Statute."

The rigidity of the FBI is unfortunately not a humorous matter. Over the years, increasingly inflexible procedures began to interfere with the agency's efficiency. The Bureau slowed down. It became hobbled by its own regulations, which included the following:

No new investigation of any significance can be initiated without prior approval by the FBI headquarters in Washington. This requirement involves lengthy communications and review, frequently consuming several days. In one recent case, the New York City Department of Investigation learned of a labor violation in which two union members were being compelled to pay a kickback to a union officer before collecting back pay awarded to them by the NLRB. One of the employees had agreed to tape record the conversation at the time of the payoff, under the surveillance of law enforcement officers. Since the case involved a Federal offense, the city agency had immediately turned it over to the U. S. Attorney's office. The payoff was scheduled to occur two days later. A request for appropriate investigative personnel was immediately presented to the FBI. At nine o'clock on the evening before the payment was scheduled, the New York office of the FBI was still awaiting clearance from Washington. The U. S. Attorney sheepishly called the City Commissioner of Investigation and asked him to reassume jurisdiction over the case so it would not be lost. The Bureau's slow procedures had ruled out any possibility of surveillance of the crucial payoff by Federal agents.

Bureau procedures usually prohibit the serving of subpoenas by FBI agents. Although agent time should obviously not be wasted chasing after witnesses, it does make sense for FBI agents to serve subpoenas under emergency conditions, particularly in connection with their own cases. It also makes sense when an agent intends to interview a witness anyway, to avoid the need for sending out a Deputy Marshal to make service, with a complete duplication of time and effort. Nevertheless, Bureau regulations prohibit agents from serving subpoenas, and they cannot and will not do so. Recently there has been some relaxing of this prohibition, but for many years Federal law enforcement efficiency was hampered by it.

The Bureau usually does not permit travel by agents outside of their assigned districts. If, for example, an agent working on an important case in New York needs to interview a witness in Miami, he cannot go there himself to ask questions based on his extensive familiarity with the case. Instead, he must write down the facts he consders relevant, describe the questions he wants asked, and send the whole thing by teletype to the Miami FBI office. If the Miami office is busy with its own cases, the request can be postponed for an extended period of time. Once the interview is conducted, it must still be written and sent back the way it came. The slowdown of investigative momentum and loss in transmission are evident.

FBI agents are prohibited from driving Bureau cars to their homes at night. Precious time is lost every day because agents must commute to the official garage to pick up automobiles for conducting interrogations or surveillances, and then return the cars to the garage at night before heading home. The waste motion can consume several hundred hours of the agent's investigative time over the course of the year.

THE BUREAU'S IMAGE

The most troublesome part of Bureau policy, however, is the concern for the public image of the agency which frequently takes precedence over its law enforcement obligations. If an investigation involves a public or political figure, the Bureau is usually reluctant to get involved. The agency does not like to be attacked in the public press or in the legislative halls. Rather than expose the Bureau to that risk, the supervisory agents simply look for an excuse not to undertake the investigation at all.

Early in 1970, Cora Walker, a courageous black lawyer who represented a cooperative grocery store in Harlem, complained to the U. S. Attorney's office that a powerful political group was threatening to put her store out of business because it would not stock products for which the group was receiving "promotional" payments from various food distributors. The alleged violators included a union representative who was also a well-known Harlem leader and another political figure who was then a member of the New York State legislature. The matter was referred to the FBI for investigation. For months the Bureau made one excuse after another for not taking the obvious steps necessary to investigate the matter adequately. The FBI disputed the existence of Federal jurisdiction as well as the violation of any statutes. Finally, the U. S. Attorney's office itself took over the investigation. Through the use of the grand jury, the office subpoenaed witnesses; an indictment was filed, followed by conviction. If the matter had been left to the FBI, it is doubtful that the case would ever have been put together.

On the other hand, the FBI is sometimes reckless in seeking publicity. The standard device is to arrange for the arrest of newsworthy defendants, who are then taken to FBI headquarters, where they can be paraded before photographers before they are taken to the courthouse. By alerting the press, the FBI has the media cover the arrival of the defendants at the agency's headquarters, then issues a press release before the defendants are taken down to court. This practice runs directly counter to the policy of not engaging in unnecessary arrests of defendants whose appearance is assured. The Bureau nevertheless insists on making arrests in newsworthy cases, to take full advantage of the opportunity for agency publicity.

Such publicity can be harmful to the public. In one case in New York, the Bureau proudly announced that it had broken up a ring engaged in the theft and sale of sixteen-millimeter prints of the motion picture *The Godfather*. When the defendants who had been arrested by the FBI were brought to the courthouse, it was obvious that one of them was innocent of any criminal involvement. The charges against him were dropped. The damage, however, had been done. The young man's name and reputation had been seriously hurt because of the premature FBI press release.

There are many more things that go into an agency's image than what happens in public. In the summer of 1970 a newly appointed U. S. Attorney, whose character and integrity had been fully checked by an FBI field investigation, paid a courtesy call on the Director. He brought his wife with him so that she could have a chance to meet the fabled head of the FBI. As the United States Attorney and his wife were being ushered into Hoover's office, an FBI agent standing by the door politely removed the wife's handbag with the comment "You won't be needing this in there." Obviously, it was a precaution against a weapon possibly concealed in the handbag. The incident did little to diminish the FBI's reputation for arrogance in its dealings with other law enforcement officials, including colleagues in the U. S. Attorneys' offices.

BUREAU OPERATIONS

In 1927, three years after J. Edgar Hoover had become Director of the then Bureau of Investigation, the entire staff consisted of some 600 persons, of whom 117 were in Washington and the balance in 33 offices across the country. In Washington there were seven divisions. The Criminal Investigative Division boasted a file of over one million fingerprint records, and during the preceding fiscal year had made a total of thirty-nine thousand fingerprint identifications. By 1972, forty-five years later, the number of FBI staff personnel had increased to over twenty thousand, operating out of the national headquarters and fifty-nine field offices. The number of fingerprints on file had increased to two hundred million, and substantially more than two million fingerprint identifications were made during the fiscal year. The number of divisions in the Bureau had increased to ten.

The major changes in the Bureau over this period were in its administrative operations, with a very rapid increase in the processing of fingerprints and other data; the preparation of uniform crime reports; and the establishment of a National Crime Information Center, which recorded information on stolen property and on fugitives sought for the commission of serious crimes, and which was connected to a communications network involving all fifty states and the Royal Canadian Mounted Police. Another major development in the Bureau was the expansion of the FBI Laboratory, whose services are now available on a cost-free basis to law enforcement agencies throughout the country, and which performs almost four hundred thousand scientific examinations during the year.

Without any question, however, the most important change in the makeup and operation of the FBI has come about because of its entry into domestic-intelligence-gathering for national security purposes. This function was unknown to the Bureau when it was first organized. Since that fateful conversation at the White House in 1936 between President Roosevelt and Director Hoover, the work of the FBI in the national security area has increased many times over. These activities include coordination and dissemination of security data among various agencies in the executive branch, and the conduct of background checks on applicants for sensitive government positions. Thousands of agents are engaged in this work.

The FBI today undoubtedly has the widest statutory jurisdiction for investigating Federal offenses of all the enforcement agencies, covering 180 categories of violations. The Bureau generally boasts about its work in organized crime—which is primarily limited to gambling prosecutions—and its operations in the following areas of criminal law enforcement:

> Bank robberies
> Other bank crimes
> Fraud against the Government
> Stolen property
> Stolen cars
> Cargo thefts
> Civil rights
> Federal lands
> Assaults on police
> Bombs

In recent years the FBI has concentrated on solving robberies, airplane hijackings, property thefts, illegal gambling, and other violations where there is a clear distinction between "good guy" and "bad guy." Depending heavily on informants, the Bureau investigates these cases by a fairly cut-and-dried procedure of interviewing all available witnesses, conducting laboratory tests where appropriate, and then making arrests if a violation has been established. Not surprisingly, the best of the FBI investigative squads are the hijacking, fugitive, and bank-robbery squads. There is little strength in the Bureau's investigative resources for dealing with fraud, corruption, obstruction of justice, perjury, civil rights offenses, and similar sophisticated violations, which are more controversial and more difficult to investigate and prosecute. The FBI is proud of its high volume of convictions and its long prison sentences, but agents seldom discuss their results in the type of offense that requires initiative or special sophistication, which go to the heart of maintaining the integrity of modern American government and society.

THE FBI'S VIEW OF ITS ROLE

When Attorney General George W. Wickersham went into office in 1909, he began working with the new Bureau of Investigation in the Justice Department. Two decades later, in his final report to President Herbert Hoover on proposals to improve enforcement of the criminal laws of the United States, Wickersham wrote:

> The closest cooperation must exist between officers charged with the detection of offenses and preparation of evidence on the one hand, and the United States Attorneys and their Assistants, who prosecute the cases, on the other hand.

Unfortunately, that close cooperation has largely disappeared. The FBI, although nominally part of the Department of Justice, operates essentially as an independent entity. When it comes to the United States Attorneys' offices, the Bureau decides what cases it will investigate and how. It generally assumes an aloof posture in maintaining a distinction between the investigative and the prosecutive functions. *We* will investigate the cases, says the FBI, and *you* can then prosecute them.

Although there is a superficial appeal to the argument that trained investigators can handle the investigation of crime better than lawyers, the logic of the argument quickly disappears when you get down to cases. It would be one thing if the FBI investigated every allegation that was brought to its attention, and did so vigorously. But this, alas, is not so. The FBI has a fixation on questions of "jurisdiction" and will not investigate cases that are at all close to the jurisdictional line, no matter how serious the facts of the offense. Before taking on an investigative assignment, the Bureau wants to know what section of the Federal code has been violated and by whom. Often the Bureau insists on a full delineation of the "proof" before the investigation is even begun. Otherwise the agency will simply refuse to go forward.

Even when the FBI does undertake an investigation, it often views its job as ending at the courthouse door. When the U. S. Attorney needs help in locating additional evidence or interviewing witnesses, that is frequently regarded as his problem. The Bureau agent generally assumes that he has completed his part of the job with the filing of the indictment. The rest is up to the Assistant U. S. Attorney.

Not long ago, the United States Attorney's office in New York was asked by the SEC to assist in an important securities fraud investigation. As the investigation developed, several of the prospective defendants attempted to obstruct the inquiry, and threatening letters and telephone calls were made to one of the key witnesses. Since the prospective defendant was now a potential Federal witness, the matter was obviously within the jurisdiction of the FBI, whose investigative responsibility includes obstruction of justice. When the FBI was asked to investigate the matter, the agency declined, on the ground that the case had originated with the SEC and that it was therefore *their* problem to investigate threats against the witness. What makes the reponse so preposterous is that the SEC has no trained investigative staff that can look into threats of violence. The SEC investigators are primarily lawyers, accountants, and securities specialists. Nonetheless, the FBI stubbornly held to its view, and prevailed.

An unusual example of the adversary role of the FBI in relation to the U. S. Attorney's office occurred early in 1973, when the Bureau's New York office became involved in a dispute between the Southern and Eastern districts of New York over the conduct of a narcotics investigation. The Narcotics Unit in the Southern District had been conducting a far-ranging investigation into an international heroin-smuggling operation that may have been connected to organized crime. The case had originally been developed in the Southern District through the cooperation of a fugitive who had been arrested in Brazil, and involved a substantial shipment of heroin which had been picked up in Manhattan and delivered in Brooklyn. Because both districts were involved, an unfortunate tug-of-war developed between two Assistant U. S. Attorneys who were investigating related aspects of the case. While efforts were being made to straighten out the competition, news arrived that an alien picked up in Brazil was being deported to Italy via New York. Federal narcotics agents obtained seats on the plane that was bringing the suspect to New York. A sealed indictment was filed in the Southern District and a warrant was issued to authorize the arrest of the alien when he crossed into U. S. territory. Since Kennedy Airport is located in the Eastern District, the Assistant U. S. Attorney in that office saw his chance to intercept the alien and interrogate him himself. Unknown to the Southern District office, the Eastern Distrct enlisted the assistance of the FBI, who had men waiting at the airport as the alien was marched off the plane in custody of the narcotics agents, who already had him under arrest. He was immediately placed in a waiting Marshal's van and transported to the courthouse in Manhattan. The FBI agents were irate, and a report flashed to Washington. L. Patrick Gray III, the Acting Director of the FBI, then filed a detailed written complaint with the

Attorney General against the Southern District U. S. Attorney's office. So distorted were the factual statements in the complaint that the FBI's Assistant Director in New York called up to apologize. But one thing was clear from the incident and many others like it: the FBI does not consider itself obligated to provide "the closest cooperation" unless it feels like it.

One of the most serious problems in the FBI's approach to criminal law enforcement has been its almost complete refusal to conduct undercover investigations. The standard procedure for FBI investigative work is to have a team of agents conduct field interviews and occasionally surveillance. When it comes to infiltrating criminal conspiracies, the FBI bows out. The primary FBI source for inside information is informants. These are usually small-time criminals who provide information to FBI agents in return for a measure of protection from prosecution, and frequently also for cash. Informants are sometimes useful for the purposes of initiating investigations, and their value should not be underestimated. The problem with the Bureau's extensive reliance on such people, however, is the debilitating effect it has on the agents themselves. The agents come to rely on the informants to do the dirty work, while they stay back on the sidelines. This means that the agents frequently become so dependent on underworld sources that they overlook conduct that is questionable. Sometimes they will not prosecute cases against known violators where the result might be the identification of their informant.

While relying almost completely on criminals and their associates for information, the Bureau is totally opposed to polygraph testing. The "lie-detector" test has not yet reached the level of general legal admissibility as evidence, but in the hands of the skilled operator it is an extremely important tool. Although a polygraph may not be 100 percent accurate when it indicates that a person is telling the *truth*, it is virtually 100 percent accurate in establishing that he is *lying*. In other words, an informant making a false statement can invariably be unmasked by a skillful polygraph operator. The psychological value of the device in criminal investigations is extremely significant. The failure of the FBI to make use of this instrument, particularly when the agency relies so heavily on information provided by persons of dubious credibility, is hard to justify.

The FBI is a loner in criminal investigations. It simply will not work in close cooperation with any other investigative office. The reasons are largely narcissistic, although the Bureau attempts to rationalize it on the basis of security and integrity. As a result, FBI agents frequently hold back information that can be valuable to other Federal or state agencies. Because of the FBI's secretiveness, these other agencies are reluctant to turn over their information to the Bureau. "It's always a one-way street" is the typical complaint of local police departments when they speak of Bureau cooperation. FBI agents are always seeking information, but they never give any in return.

Other law enforcement agencies have repeatedly demonstrated that effective cooperation is possible. For example, excellent work has been carried out between the New York City Police Department and the Federal narcotics enforcement agencies. When it comes to participation from the FBI, such cooperation is generally nonexistent.

For many years the refusal of the Bureau to share information even with other Federal agencies proved to be a stumbling block to effective enforcement activities against organized crime. This foot-dragging was dealt a substantial blow when Robert F. Kennedy was Attorney General. The device he used was simplicity itself. He proposed that the U. S. Attorney's office for the Southern District of New York establish a master file, with a card entry for every report from any investigative source cross-indexed according to the names of figures engaged in organized criminal activity. Any recognized Federal agency working in the organized crime field was given access to this index. With one stroke, all of the contents of the FBI files were made available to other Federal agencies, and their files were also opened to the Bureau. This has been the concept behind the Department of Justice's Joint Strike Forces against Organized Crime—to pool resources and intelligence in order to do a better job.

Notwithstanding the establishment of the Joint Strike Forces against Organized Crime, the Bureau still continued to go it alone, offering only token participation. This led one Strike Force attorney to comment, whenever another instance of FBI obstructionism or delay appeared in an investigation: "If the mob only knew!"

Shortly after he became Acting Director of the FBI, L. Patrick Gray III issued a message to all law enforcement officials in the FBI *Law Enforcement Bulletin.*

> There are many evils which can and do afflict our profession. None is worse than corruption. There can be no room for corruption in the ranks of the law enforcement profession. Corruption erodes the public trust and confidence which is the foundation of our profession. . . . Well-meaning platitudes condemning isolated instances of corruption in law enforcement do little to correct the problem. What is needed is strong leadership to expose and take action against each case of corruption.

The Organized Crime Control Act of 1970 for the first time gave the Federal Government direct and specific jurisdiction to investigate and prosecute local police corruption. Shortly after the act went into effect, the U. S. Attorney's office in New York and representatives of the New York office of the FBI met to discuss techniques to use in carrying out the congressional mandate to prosecute local corruption. FBI personnel produced a series of maps indicating the principal concentrations of known gambling activities in the city. Such known gambling operations cannot flourish without police protection. The problem was how to go about investigating and bringing corruption to an end.

Possible techniques were suggested by the experienced Assistant U. S. Attorneys present at the conference: surveillance of known gambling operations; undercover work on the inside; interrogation of police officers on whose beats gambling operations were found to be wide open. The chief FBI representative at the conference simply commented that the Bureau would not engage in any "fishing expeditions." Despite repeated efforts to get the Bureau to move thereafter, nothing happened. As far as the Bureau was concerned, there was no police corruption in New York City, and nothing to investigate.

Then came the Knapp Commission, created in response to a series of newspaper stories quoting police officers about the widespread pattern of police corruption in the city. Though it was only a temporary agency with limited resources, the Knapp Commission was able in a very short time to turn up evidence of widespread police corruption. The commission's chief counsel, Michael Armstrong, and some of the members of the staff were alumni of the Southern District U. S. Attorney's office.

A series of important breaks occurred. Several police officers agreed to cooperate with the Knapp Commission. One of them was Robert Leuci, well acquainted with widespread corruption in local enforcement of the narcotics laws. Leuci, a New York City narcotics detective, was turned over to the U. S. Attorney's office for development of investigative leads. A brand-new Official Corruption Unit was created within the office to coordinate the investigations under Edward M. Shaw. A member of the Knapp Commission staff, Nicholas Scoppetta, was quietly sworn in as a Special Assistant U. S. Attorney. In contrast to the FBI's unwillingness to investigate police corruption, investigative assistance was given without limitation by the Federal Bureau of Narcotics and Dangerous Drugs and, later, by the New York City Police Department itself. A series of important corruption cases resulted.

The extent of local police corruption in narcotics enforcement was stunning. The NYC Police Department had established a Special Investigating Unit consisting of seventy-four

111

police officers charged with tracking down major narcotics dealers and wholesalers. After Federal and state investigations got under way, eighteen of these SIU officers were indicted on criminal charges, two shot themselves, and many others were the subject of investigations or departmental proceedings, all growing out of shakedowns and bribes related to narcotics enforcement activities. The lieutenant in charge of SIU was indicted and convicted of Federal income-tax evasion for failing to report $65,260 in "outside income" received in one year alone.

The Knapp Commission also provided informants and witnesses to help develop Federal prosecutions against corrupt police officers protecting illegal gambling operations. The very first Federal prosecution under the Organized Crime Control Act of 1970 for violation of the section against corruption of local police officers was actually filed in the Southern District of New York, but not because of any investigative activity by the FBI. It was because of cooperation from the temporary New York City investigating commission, which had shown enough initiative and enterprise to develop the proof that had been there all the time.

A number of factors explain the failure of the FBI to show more creativity in its investigative work in the sensitive areas of corruption and white-collar crime. Some believe that the failure of the Bureau to investigate police corruption stems from the desire of Bureau agents not to offend their counterparts in local law enforcement agencies. The deeper reason for the loss of initiative has undoubtedly been that the stultified policies of the FBI in its later years destroyed the creativity and sense of righteous indignation that had characterized the agency in its prime. Although it has built the best criminal-intelligence network of any law enforcement agency in the country, the Bureau shows no imagination at all when it comes to criminal investigations based on that intelligence. The institutionalized thinking of the FBI field offices is that the agency must be provided with a specific allegation showing a clear Federal law violation before the Bureau can initiate an investigation. In contrast to this attitude, various U. S. Attorneys' offices, even though largely staffed by young lawyers with limited law enforcement experience, repeatedly demonstrate remarkable enterprise and energy in developing investigative approaches to root out unlawful conduct.

PLAYING BALL WITH THE WHITE HOUSE

The enlargement of the FBI's jurisdiction in 1936 to include domestic-intelligence-gathering for national security purposes opened a direct line of communication between the FBI and the White House. Whereas investigation of criminal matters primarily involves working with the Attorney General and the U. S. Attorneys, national security questions involve matters of direct concern to the President and his staff. Expansion of this responsibility—to include coordination of national security intelligence background investigations of candidates for sensitive posts—involved closer identification with the interests of the White House. The net result was to bind the Director of the FBI and the agency itself more closely to those whose political interests often affect their judgments of the way government agencies should function.

During the early stages of the Teapot Dome scandal, a United States Senator issued a warning that now seems almost prophetic. Senator Thomas J. Walsh, head of the Senate investigation into oil-lease irregularities, met with special prosecutor Owen J. Roberts shortly after Roberts's selection by President Coolidge. After Roberts explained his mission, Walsh said, "I have only one piece of advice. I wouldn't depend on the Justice Department for investigative purposes, nor would I approach the Attorney General's office for information if I were you." Senator Walsh proceeded to explain the relationship between

Harry Daugherty and others in the Harding Administration and expressed the suspicion that Daugherty himself might have been involved in the scandal. "In addition," the Senator continued, "the Department of Justice and its Bureau of Investigation are handpicked by Daugherty and rotten to the core."

A half-century later, during a taped conversation with his counsel, John Dean, on March 13, 1973, President Nixon discussed the use of the FBI for political investigative purposes by prior Administrations and spoke of developing a similar relationship with the FBI under its new Director, L. Patrick Gray III. The President and his counsel talked about the possibility that Gray's confirmation might be delayed until after the Watergate hearings were completed. The following conversation ensued:

> *Nixon:* That's a vote really for us, because Gray, in my opinion, should not be the head of the FBI. After going through the hell of the hearings, he will not be a good Director, as far as we are concerned.

> *Dean:* I think that is true. I think he will be a very suspect Director. Not that I don't think Pat won't do what we want—I do look at him a little differently than Dick [Kleindienst] in that regard. Like he is still keeping in close touch with me. He is calling me. He has given me his hot line. We talk at night, how do you want me to handle this, et cetera? So he still stays in touch, and is still being involved, but he can't do it because he is going to be under such surveillance by his own people —every move he is making—that it would be a difficult thing for Pat. Not that Pat wouldn't want to play ball, but he may not be able to.

> *Nixon:* I agree. That's what I meant.

The prospect of any FBI Director's "playing ball" with the White House on investigative matters is chilling. And yet apparently that reality has existed to some extent with all three recent directors of the FBI.

The most shocking example occurred when Gray, as Acting Director of the FBI while that agency was supposed to be investigating the Watergate cover-up, turned over to Dean, who was coordinating the cover-up operations, the confidential results of the FBI's investigation. Dean knew what was being learned by the investigators, and could plan the countermoves accordingly. Gray also arranged for Dean to sit in on all of the FBI interviews of White House personnel, insuring the safety of the concealment plan.

Gray turned over FBI investigative reports to Dean without informing or consulting the Attorney General or the Assistant Attorney General in charge of the Watergate investigation. He explained his reasons in his subsequent testimony before the Ervin Committee:

Q. Now, Mr. Gray, did you consult with Mr. Petersen and Mr. Kleindienst about the advisability of giving the F.B.I. data to Mr. Dean?

A. No, sir, I did not.

Q. Why did you not?

A. I didn't do it because I thought I was the Acting Director of the Federal Bureau of Investigation and when I have a request from the Counsel to the President of the United States I don't have to go run around to the Attorney General and to the Assistant Attorney General in charge of the Criminal Division and ask them to hold my hand and help me respond in making a decision. I did not do that and I would not do that.

Q. I don't mean to quibble with you but you had 26 years of military experience and you know things about the chain of command. You didn't work for Mr. Dean, did you? Your direct supervisor and your boss, so to speak, was Mr. Kleindienst, wasn't it?

A. That is correct. And also the President of the United States is my boss and when the Counsel to the

115

President levies a request upon me, I am going to comply
with that request and I did comply with it.

And so the conflict between the obligation to investigate
violations of law fairly and impartially and a feeling of loyalty
to the administration in power is baldly portrayed.

The extent to which loyalty to the White House can subvert
the judgment and actions of the Director of the Federal Bureau
of Investigation was spelled out in the most dramatic aspect of
Gray's testimony. This time he described to the Ervin Committee how he accepted without question politically sensitive
documents removed from the files of one of the Watergate defendants, turned over to him by two of the President's top
assistants.

> I asked whether these files should become a part of
> our F.B.I. Watergate file. Mr. Dean said these should not
> become a part of our F.B.I. Watergate file, but that he
> wanted to be able to say, if called upon later, that he had
> turned all of Howard Hunt's files over to the F.B.I.
> I distinctly recall Mr. Dean saying that these files were
> "political dynamite," and "clearly should not see the
> light of day."
> It is true that neither Mr. Ehrlichman nor Mr. Dean
> expressly instructed me to destroy the files. But there
> was, and is, no doubt in my mind that destruction was
> intended.

In fact Gray did destroy the files the following December,
when he burned the household trash at his home in Connecticut. But not until after he had looked at the documents. When,
a few months later, Assistant Attorney General Petersen came
to see him and told him that Dean had advised the Assistant
U. S. Attorney in the Watergate investigation that he, Dean,
had turned over two of Hunt's files to Gray, Gray lied. He said
that he had never received the files. Overnight he had a change
of heart, and the following day he told Petersen part of the
truth, although he still lied in saying that he had not looked at

116

the files themselves. Ultimately, reluctantly, Gray told the truth, once he was caught. What would have happened if Dean had never come forward and talked?

The willingness of the Director of the FBI to "play ball" with the White House in political matters apparently was not limited to Acting Director Gray. Presidential aide Haldeman admitted in testimony before the Ervin Committee that an investigation of CBS newsman Daniel Schorr had been conducted by the FBI. J. Edgar Hoover, who had ordered the investigation at the White House's request, had falsely advised Senator Ervin that the investigation was in fact a background check for a possible government appointment, even though Hoover wrote in a confidential memorandum that he was aware of the falsity of this statement. In the course of 1975 testimony before the House Subcommittee on Civil Rights, Attorney General Levi revealed that Presidents Kennedy, Johnson and Nixon had all requested the FBI to conduct investigations of Congressmen.

The House Judiciary Committee, during its impeachment inquiry, discovered that the FBI had, at White House request, placed seventeen "national-security" wiretaps, without court orders, in an attempt to halt leaks of government information. Targets of the wiretaps included four newsmen and thirteen government officials, at least three of whom had no known access to national security material. Director Hoover also sent wiretap information to the White House indicating that former Defense Secretary Clark Clifford intended to write a magazine article criticizing the Vietnam policies of the Nixon Administration. Wiretap information concerning a conversation containing uncomplimentary remarks about Mr. Kissinger was also supplied by the FBI to Kissinger when he was on the White House staff.

Apparently, even the current Director of the FBI is willing to follow White House orders. When Archibald Cox was fired for his insistence on pursuing a subpoena for the White House tapes, Director Clarence M. Kelley instructed FBI agents to seal off the Special Prosecutor's offices and block all access to Professor Cox and members of his staff. When the FBI agents later did permit the lawyers to enter, the attorneys were prevented from removing anything—one lawyer was even stopped from taking home a photograph of his wife. Simultaneously, the FBI took control of the Justice Department files of former Attorney General Elliot L. Richardson and former Deputy Attorney General William D. Ruckelshaus, both of whom had resigned to protest Cox's dismissal. The FBI's seizure had all the earmarks of secret-police action, and plainly was a misuse of the agency by the White House.

In his laudatory book *The F.B.I. Story,* Donald Whitehead rejected the possibility that the Bureau could ever become a secret police similar to that in Nazi Germany. Yet he sounded one word of caution:

> But there is one condition under which the FBI could become a "Gestapo." This could happen if the traditional checks and restraints were corrupted or eliminated by a dictatorial government, and the FBI was then used as a political tool.

The close relationship between the White House and the FBI brought about by its intelligence-gathering and national security work has undercut the traditional checks and restraints that help guarantee the impartiality of the agency. To the extent that the FBI has let itself be used as a political tool by the White House, Federal law enforcement is in trouble. A way must be found to separate those Bureau functions answerable to the President's staff from traditional criminal investigative work. The latter must be subject to only one standard—even-handed, impartial justice that favors no man, whatever his station.

6

POLITICIZING
NARCOTICS ENFORCEMENT

By the end of the nineteen-sixties, heroin addiction in the United States had reached epidemic proportions. Estimates of the number of active addicts ranged as high as six hundred thousand. Heroin addiction had long since expanded beyond the limits of the inner city. Many middle-income and wealthy young people had been hooked. The crime level had soared, particularly for crimes related to quick dollar turnover to finance narcotics needs—burglaries, muggings, robberies of stores. Everywhere people were blaming the law enforcement agencies for failing to stop the drug problem. The strongest criticism was leveled at the Federal law enforcement agencies, since they had primary jurisdiction over international traffic operations.

When I took office as United States Attorney for the Southern District of New York, in 1970, I was determined to give top priority to effective narcotics enforcement. The existing staff of four Assistant U. S. Attorneys in the Narcotics Unit was expanded. By 1973, ten lawyers worked full time on narcotics enforcement in the Southern District alone. A number of other Assistants helped out with the trial of specific cases. As U. S. Attorney, I participated actively in enforcement-planning and prosecution activity, and personally tried a major international narcotics-smuggling case—the first time a United States Attorney had done so in the district in at least ten years.

The emphasis on Federal narcotics enforcement was echoed on the national level. The Attorney General announced narcotics roundups in various metropolitan centers. He personally negotiated with French officials to establish enforcement-cooperation agreements. The White House became increasingly interested in the subject. The Bureau of Narcotics and Dangerous Drugs, under a vigorous new chief, John E. Ingersoll, was rebuilding its resources and operations. The number of special agents in the Bureau jumped from 884 in 1970 to 1,610 in 1972. Almost half of them were stationed in foreign countries, at fifty-seven different locations. Meanwhile, the budget for Federal narcotics enforcement increased from $78 million in 1970 to $729 million requested for 1973.

Sensing the political importance of the narcotics issue, President Nixon became increasingly visible in enforcement activities. Publicly calling drug abuse "Public Enemy No. 1," he announced several new programs to combat narcotics traffic and addiction. He created a Special Action Office for Drug Abuse Prevention and established a cabinet-level International Narcotics Control Committee with Secretary of State William Rogers as chairman.

In 1970, the U. S. Attorney's office for the Southern District of New York had compiled a list of known narcotics distributors and submitted it to the Internal Revenue Service. We requested that a special program of tax audits be instituted in an effort to bring these violators to justice. By 1971, the idea had been taken over as a national program of the Internal Revenue Service, and by 1972 the White House was seeking special funds for additional IRS agents to carry on the work.

Other Federal agencies were brought into the narcotics effort, including the Law Enforcement Assistance Administration, the Postal Service, the Office of Education, the National Institute of Mental Health, the Department of Defense, and the Department of State.

An important part of the new national attention on narcotics enforcement was an increased emphasis on education and treatment. I had become concerned about the lack of attention to treatment and education and had written a book on the subject.* Not satisfied with the rate of Federal rehabilitation efforts, the Southern District initiated its own rehabilitation program. But enforcement continued to be the major ingredient in the Federal narcotics effort. That is where the hardest work had to be done.

Probably the most significant development in this stepped-up narcotics enforcement effort was the cooperative working relationship built up between Federal and local narcotics agencies. The first dramatic results were disclosed on April 17, 1973. The Southern District of New York announced the filing of *nine* indictments charging *seventy-one* defendants with violations of the Federal narcotics and income-tax laws. Simultaneously, the District of New Jersey filed a separate indictment charging *sixteen* defendants with violations of the Federal narcotics laws. Additional indictments were filed in the Eastern District of New York and in the New York State courts. This whole complex of cases produced a nationwide crackdown on the wholesale narcotics distribution network that had the capacity to process a hundred kilograms of heroin every three or four weeks.

This group of joint narcotics prosecutions culminated a two-year investigation that had been initiated by the New York City Police Department in April, 1971. Because of the expanding scope and complexity of the investigation, the Police Department was later joined in its work by the New York Joint Task Force, a combined Federal-state effort, and Federal narcotics investigators. During the final six months of the investigation a

---

* *The Young Die Quietly: The Narcotics Problem in America* (New York, William Morrow, 1972).

total of 159 law enforcement officers from various agencies were made available for the investigation. The investigation was coordinated by Anthony Pohl, of the Federal Bureau of Narcotics and Dangerous Drugs, and Assistant U. S. Attorney Gerald A. Feffer, from the Southern District of New York. During the investigation, thirty-two court-ordered wiretaps and eavesdropping orders were obtained; seven state and three Federal search warrants were executed; and extensive photographing and videotaping of meetings and narcotics transactions took place.

The joint Federal-city investigative effort continued to produce dramatic results with the indictment, on October 4, 1973, of forty-three more narcotics violators, including Carmine Tramunti, widely identified as the head of the Thomas Luchese crime family. The Tramunti case was subsequently tried by United States Attorney Paul J. Curran, who had been a member of the Narcotics Unit in the Southern District of New York during his earlier service as an Assistant U. S. Attorney. In his summation to the jury, Mr. Curran described Tramunti as the "chairman of the board" of a huge enterprise that distributed massive amounts of heroin on the streets of New York City. Reflecting on the importance of the joint operation in assembling sufficient evidence to warrant prosecution, Mr. Curran observed, "Someone of Tramunti's stature would never be caught touching narcotics. Carmine Tramunti doesn't handle narcotics any more than Henry Ford works on the assembly line." After five days of deliberation, the jury returned a guilty verdict against Tramunti and fourteen other defendants. Among the major defendants convicted in the case were Joseph DiNapoli, Frank Pugliese, and Angelo Mamone.

The net result of all of this effort has been impressive. In the Southern District of New York alone, narcotics indictments rose from 15 percent of the total number of criminal cases in 1963 to almost 29 percent in 1973. The number of defendants more than quadrupled, from 243 to 991. More significantly, the stature of the defendants within the narcotics operations increased sharply. The result of the enforcement effort was felt on the streets of New York and elsewhere. For a sustained period of time the supply of heroin began to diminish. By 1974 officials estimated that the six hundred thousand heroin addicts in 1970 had been cut back to between a hundred and fifty and three hundred thousand. Others had moved into various forms of treatment, including methadone, and still others had either given up their addiction or turned to soft drugs and alcohol.

The impact of this intense period of effective law enforcement on the supply of heroin was clear. But it was by no means complete, and never will be as long as a black market exists. The profits are so high and the incessant need of heroin addicts so great that the pressure of drug demand will continue to be a threat. Nevertheless, anyone connected with Federal law enforcement could take great pride in the combined achievements of the Federal narcotics agents and the United States Attorneys' offices in this major crackdown on narcotics traffickers.

THE MANPOWER

It was a strange sight. Along both sides of the narrow street in the lower-middle-income suburb of Wood-Ridge, New Jersey, stood two lines of solemn-faced Federal narcotics agents facing each other. The day was October 16, 1972, and it was chilly and overcast. Many of the agents appeared completely out of place. They wore long hair or whiskers and would have looked more at home in Washington Square or a hippie hangout. But every one of them was standing erect with a gold badge in its leather case hanging from a breast pocket: "Special Agent —Bureau of Narcotics and Dangerous Drugs."

A crowd of only two or three hundred, mostly neighbors and representatives of other police and law enforcement organizations, lined up behind the rows of agents on each side of the street. As they stood there, the funeral procession slowly made its way toward the gray-stone Assumption Roman Catholic Church. The shiny black hearse stopped in front of the church door and an honor guard of granite-faced agents opened the rear door of the hearse, lifted out the coffin containing the body of Frank Tummillo, and carried it into the church. The crowd followed. Agents lined the walls of the church. Every seat was filled. Frank's parents sat dazed and unbelieving in the front pew. His fiancée, Carla Starita, whom he had intended to marry in that same church in less than a month, occasionally broke into sobs.

I could feel the special sense of pride and shared grief that ran through the congregation. The feeling of personal danger, so dramatically underlined in Frank Tummillo's death, helped to tie the special bonds of what was, for a brief moment, one of the most remarkable law enforcement organizations ever to work together in Federal service.

The funeral service itself was simple. The parish priest conveyed his compassion in the simple service and in his words of consolation to the parents. Director Ingersoll delivered a eulogy that spoke more to the living agents than of the dead man lying in the coffin. He reminded the agents, through his praise of Frank Tummillo, that they were engaged in hazardous professional work in the nation's service, and that they should be proud of what they were doing.

Frank Tummillo represented the new type of Federal narcotics agent brought in during Director Ingersoll's remaking of the agency. After graduating from St. Francis College in Loretto, Pennsylvania, in 1968, Frank had gone directly to work for BNDD. There he had been shaped into a special agent in a unit supervised by Robert Manning, also a St. Francis graduate, who had recruited Frank and other college graduates. Frank was one of his stars.

Frank Tummillo's specialty was undercover work. He was

regarded as a natural. Only five and a half feet tall, he had dark hair, and had grown a "Fu Manchu" moustache to help him bridge the gap between his role as a law enforcement officer and the hippie world in which he had to be accepted to be effective as an undercover agent. After four years of training, Frank Tummillo was transferred to a new squad, headed by a resourceful professional, Thomas Devine, who, at the age of thirty, had become something of a legend for his toughness and ingenuity as a narcotics-enforcement field commander. His father, Bill Devine, had for many years served as a detective in the office of Frank Hogan, District Attorney of New York County. Both Devines had committed their lives to upholding the law, and to doing so with fortitude, good humor, and decency.

Tom Devine's squad received a tip from an informant that a man named Jose Nieves was dealing in substantial quantities of cocaine, which was being smuggled from Argentina. Devine decided to assign an undercover agent to make contact with Nieves to see if it would be possible to buy some of the cocaine. Frank Tummillo was assigned the job and in no time made contact with Nieves and opened negotiations. Nieves agreed to sell Tummillo ten kilograms of cocaine for a hundred and sixty thousand dollars. On the evening of October 12, 1972, Jose Nieves and a friend, Jose Mattos, went to room 1007 of the Sheraton Motor Inn on the West Side of Manhattan. There they met with Frank Tummillo and another undercover agent. They counted a hundred and sixty thousand dollars in bills that the two Federal agents had with them. The cocaine sellers left, saying they would be back in an hour and a half with "the goods." Apparently they changed their minds. Instead of delivering the cocaine, they returned three-quarters of an hour later with pistols. They caught Frank Tummillo off guard as he was about to leave the room to join the other agents who had staked out the motel. From the adjoining room, Tom Devine heard a commotion and came through the connecting door. He was hit by a hail of bullets, one of which struck him in the back just below the neck as he fell forward. During the shooting Frank Tummillo was killed. As the two suspects tried to make their escape, they ran into narcotics agents in the hallway, who came running when they heard the gunfire. Both suspects fell dead, one with seven bullets in his body, the other with four.

For Frank Tummillo, aged twenty-five, the story ended there. But for Tom Devine, things were different. The shot in the neck paralyzed him from the chest down and left him a cripple for the rest of his life. His courageous wife, mother of two small children, met the challenge with remarkable strength. After many months in the hospital at a special therapy center, Tom Devine went home and then started back to work at BNDD, where he still serves as a symbol of that special fortitude of which heroes are made. In 1974, a group of public-spirited citizens chipped in to buy him a new house, specially designed to facilitate his restricted movements.

Thomas Devine, Frank Tummillo, and Robert Manning were part of the rejuvenation of the Federal Bureau of Narcotics after corruption scandals had clouded the agency in 1967 and 1968. The administration of BNDD under its new director, John Ingersoll, emphasized integrity, teamwork, and professionalism. Previously, the emphasis had been on individual ingenuity and guts, with few controls and little accountability.

The popular view of the old-style narcotics agents is reflected in the film *The French Connection*. A New York City narcotics detective is portrayed as an arrogant bully, who does not hesitate to walk into a Harlem bar and violate the civil rights of every patron in the place. Such characters produce colorful stories. But there was another, corrupt side to such stories. John Ingersoll was determined that this would not happen to the Bureau of Narcotics and Dangerous Drugs.

To insure the integrity of the new Bureau of Narcotics and

Dangerous Drugs, Ingersoll's men concentrated on recruiting young agents with excellent records. The principal BNDD personnel recruiter in the New York region followed this order of preference: first choice, captains from the Marine Corps; second choice, lieutenants from the Navy; third choice, captains from the Army. His recruiting theory, which proved correct time and again, was that men emerging from the service had a strong sense of loyalty to the Federal Government, were seasoned in combat training, were in good health, and were likely to have an aversion to corruption. An absolute rule in BNDD was never to hire a former policeman or detective, since there was no way to guarantee that he had not been corrupted or had not developed associations that could comprise his integrity while working on the street.

Narcotics investigators, particularly those who work under cover, deal with the worst elements of society, constantly handling large sums of cash and transacting business with men who must live by their wits. The temptation to go bad is particularly strong in the narcotics field. Even narcotics detectives who simply participate in arrests are subject to severe temptation. It is hard for a man with a wife and children trying to live on a civil servant's salary to turn down an offer of fifty thousand dollars in cash to free a suspect, or to change his testimony at a pretrial hearing, thereby providing grounds for an order excluding seized narcotics from evidence.

Although the new recruits brought into BNDD between 1968 and 1970 were all relatively inexperienced, the planning of Ingersoll, his deputy Andrew Tartaglino, and their colleagues proved highly effective. The number of pounds of heroin seized by BNDD agents more than doubled between 1970 and 1971. So did arrests of narcotics suspects, both in the United States and abroad. In marked contrast to the employees of the FBI, the investigators and prosecutors in Federal narcotics law enforcement worked together as an effective team.

INTERNATIONAL NARCOTICS CONTROL

John Ingersoll's contributions to Federal narcotics enforcement were not limited to reorganization and strengthening of the narcotics enforcement agency. He also became the personal representative of the United States in persuading French enforcement officials to crack down on heroin-processing laboratories in Marseilles. Furthermore, he opened the way for the successful negotiations that at least temporarily halted the cultivation of opium poppies in Turkey.

Ingersoll's predecessor, Harold J. Anslinger, dominated Federal narcotics enforcement for a full generation. He was in his way as much of an institution as J. Edgar Hoover. Anslinger adopted the repressive enforcement policies that frightened doctors away from attempting to treat addicts. Anslinger, implacably opposed to treatment programs, emphasized enforcement and imprisonment and undoubtedly contributed indirectly to the acceleration of narcotics addiction and traffic. Although it had been apparent for years that a principal link in the chain of international narcotics traffic was the laboratories in Marseilles, Anslinger had never made any serious effort to enlist French police cooperation in closing them down.

The new man on the job, John Ingersoll, made cooperation with France and Turkey his first order of business. Within four or five weeks of taking office, he visited both countries, to urge them to shut down opium cultivation and heroin processing.

Ingersoll's early negotiations with the Turks were frustrating. With the assistance of the U. S. ambassador, Ingersoll met various Government officials and finally held a midnight confrontation with the Prime Minister, Suleyman Demirel. The Prime Minister was equivocal. He was concerned with the economic impact on the Turkish farmers and ensuing political consequences of a total ban. Despite strong entreaties, the Prime

Minister simply would not commit himself beyond a pledge to reduce gradually the area under opium cultivation. The negotiations ground to a halt. Shortly afterward, while in Germany, Ingersoll heard that President Sunay of Turkey was visiting in Stuttgart. The Turkish President had a reputation for being a reasonable man who would do what he believed to be the right thing. Ingersoll, accompanied by one of the BNDD special agents who had been stationed in Turkey and knew the language—and the President's son—set off through the night until he reached Stuttgart and the President. Ingersoll pushed his way past various functionaries and found himself in the presence of the President of Turkey. The two men talked together for half an hour. The President told Ingersoll that he had never heard of the U. S. proposal to provide increased financial aid in return for a halt in poppy cultivation. He said the idea made sense.

That was the turning point. Not long afterward there was a new Premier in Turkey and, with the support of the President, the new Premier worked out an agreement with the U. S. State Department under which increased AID funds would be sent to Turkey if the cultivation of the opium poppy was halted. The ban continued through Ingersoll's term as Director of BNDD.

Ingersoll's tenacity was the major factor in achieving cooperation with the French Government in closing down heroin laboratories in Marseilles. The first step in that effort was a visit by Mr. Ingersoll to Paris, where he met with Ambassador Sargent Shriver and briefed him on the extent of the narcotics problem emanating from Marseilles. Arrangements were made for him to visit enforcement personnel in the Ministry of the Interior. Ingersoll soon found himself in a room with a bespectacled junior official seated behind a small desk. Ingersoll asked to see his superior. He made the same request to each new official in turn, until finally he reached the Minister of the Interior, Raymond Marcellin. The minister blandly informed Ingersoll that there was no narcotics problem in Marseilles. He had been repeatedly assured that this was so by his top aides. Ingersoll then described recent cases in which narcotics had been traced directly to laboratories in the Marseilles area. He bluntly told the minister that his aides had simply not been telling him the truth. The minister seemed shocked. He said that he would look into Ingersoll's charges.

Some time later, Ingersoll met with the top French police officials to present his case on the existence of heroin laboratories. These officials also told Ingersoll that they had been assured that all of the allegations of heroin production in Marseilles were fictitious. Ingersoll handed them a ten-page memorandum describing how couriers and other sources of information in narcotics cases had identified heroin shipments as coming directly from Marseilles. The French officials decided to see for themselves. They assigned a special team of police officers to the Marseilles area to conduct their own investigation and report back directly. What they found confirmed everything the American had said. A major shakeup in the police hierarchy at Marseilles followed. From that point on, complete cooperation was given to the U. S. officials. A series of joint investigations and prosecutions eventually resulted in a major breakthrough in the control of international narcotics traffic.

The man at the White House who encouraged Ingersoll's missions to Turkey and France was Patrick Moynihan. Unfortunately, Mr. Moynihan did not continue in the job. In due course the responsibility was turned over to Egil Krogh, Jr., a new White House aide, who subsequently admitted in court that he was responsible for planning the burglary at the office of Daniel Ellsberg's psychiatrist. He pleaded guilty and was disbarred. White House activities in the narcotics enforcement field had begun to take a different turn.

Meanwhile, the Special Assistant Secretary of State selected by the President to head up the State Department's international narcotics control efforts was the former Republican State Chairman from New Jersey, Nelson Gross, who was subsequently indicted by U. S. Attorney Herbert Stern's office for subornation of perjury and obstruction of justice and sentenced in 1974 to two years in prison growing out of improper solicitation of corporate political campaign contributions. The days of effective narcotics enforcement were drawing to an end.

THE 1972 PRESIDENTIAL CAMPAIGN

Myles J. Ambrose had excellent Republican Party connections in New York State when the Nixon Administration first came into office. It was not long before he was named U. S. Commissioner of Customs. The Bureau of Customs traditionally shared in narcotics enforcement, and some of its men did excellent work. Ambrose, sensing the public interest in narcotics enforcement, decided to exploit this aspect of the Bureau of Customs' responsibilities. He staged a number of special crash programs, including increased inspection operations along the Mexican border. He instituted a brief period of intense baggage examination at major airports, which produced headlines as well as irate passengers. Ambrose moved around the country frequently, making speeches wherever he could, and visiting people who enjoyed being in the company of top government officials (including a rancher in Texas who turned out to be the subject of a Federal probe).

When the White House issued an executive order in 1970 assigning top narcotics enforcement responsibility to the Bureau of Narcotics and Dangerous Drugs, Ambrose hit the roof. He went to the White House and demanded a reversal. He must have impressed the staff, for the order was soon rescinded, and Ambrose continued to make headlines with his speeches and publicity stunts.

Then, in January, 1972, U. S. Attorneys from the major cities were summoned to a conference with President Nixon. The President announced that he was signing an executive order that day to create a new Office for Drug Abuse Law Enforce-

131

ment, and that Mr. Ambrose was going to be in charge. He asked the U. S. Attorneys to assign special personnel to help Ambrose in the program. He then gave out gold-plated cufflinks to each of the U. S. Attorneys and departed with a wave.

The executive order vested Ambrose with extraordinary powers. He was given the titles Special Assistant Attorney General and Special Consultant to the President for Drug Abuse Law Enforcement. The executive order said that Ambrose's job was to "advise the President with respect to all matters relating to the more effective enforcement by all Federal agencies of laws relating to illegal drug traffic, and on methods by which the Federal Government can assist State and local governments in strengthening the enforcement of their laws relating to illegal drug traffic." The order went on to state that the new director was to recommend appropriate programs, legislation, and other measures to maximize the campaign "to stamp out illegal drug traffic through effective law enforcement."

A press release accompanying the executive order described it as a "new initiative" to marshal a wide range of government resources in a concentrated assault on the street-level heroin pusher. "Working through nine regional offices, our new program will use special grand juries to gather extensive new information concerning drug traffickers and will pool this intelligence for use by Federal, State and local law enforcement agencies."

After the White House meeting, the U. S. Attorneys were summoned to a conference room at the Department of Justice, where they met with Ambrose and Deputy Attorney General Richard Kleindienst. Ambrose explained in confidence that this was a special election-year effort and that he did not know how long the program would last after November.

To professional law enforcement people the creation of ODALE was a joke. The notion that one could use grand juries to investigate street-level narcotics crime was preposterous. Narcotics traffic is a matter for field investigative work, using surveillance and negotiated purchases to obtain physical evidence on which to base a prosecution. Investigative grand juries are suited to the investigation of white-collar crimes, official corruption, and other matters that depend on testimony and documents. Not narcotis traffic. Ambrose, himself a former Assistant U. S. Attorney, must have known that too.

The special grand jury program proved a fiasco. Street pushers created scenes in the courthouse corridors as they went through withdrawal while waiting to testify. When the pushers did appear before the grand juries, they invariably turned out to have no information of value. Typically, they received their narcotics from "Charlie," a man they met on the street corner every day. Where Charlie got the stuff they had no idea.

But the publicity machine kept grinding out press releases. The number of drug pushers who had been identified by the special grand juries was listed in the thousands. Mimicking a publicity stunt that had succeeded in Virginia, Ambrose established a "Heroin Hot Line" with a central telephone number where citizens could report alleged narcotics law violators in strict confidence. The line was used mostly by cranks.

After a while the special grand jury effort and the concentration on street-level pushers were quietly abandoned. Instead, groping for case statistics, ODALE regional directors reached out to take over important investigations that were already under way in other agencies. In New York, joint Federal-police investigations were transferred to the regional office of ODALE. All of a sudden, professionals who had been engaged in long-term investigations found themselves being pushed around by young lawyers who had been hired on a temporary basis to flesh out the campaign-year program. Some of the senior law enforcement officials simply refused to turn over information to these people, fearing security leaks and damage to the valuable work that had already been done. On frequent occasions, Ambrose had to use threats to get his way. The President's name was dropped regularly in his discussions, with implicit menace. On

133

one occasion, Anthony Pohl, assigned to coordinate "Operation Window" (which later resulted in one of the most important joint Federal-local narcotics roundups in history), was so obstinate in trying to protect the investigation that Ambrose directed him to report to Washington for a confrontation with the Attorney General. When Pohl seized the chance to present his side of the dispute, Ambrose backed down.

Meanwhile, the ODALE public-relations staff was scheduling appearances for Ambrose, who traveled around the country seeking maximum publicity for the Nixon Administration's special push in narcotics enforcement. The President himself was involved in some of these publicity efforts, and came to New York City to announce the establishment of the regional office of ODALE there, with full newspaper and television coverage.

By the time election day had come and gone, the morale of the Federal narcotics agencies was ruined. Ambrose's increasingly heavy hand had resulted in chaos. One of those who had resisted the ODALE operation was John Ingersoll, whose agency's work was being cannibalized by the ODALE people. Ambrose, once rebuffed by presidential order in narcotics enforcement, was now on top and appeared bent on vengeance. The Bureau of Customs enforcement people were pushed to the forefront. After Nixon's reelection, the White House announced the creation of a new Drug Enforcement Administration to combine BNDD and the Bureau of Customs operations. In the reorganization, Ambrose's top aide, John R. Bartels, Jr., one of those responsible for generating inter-agency feuding, was to be named head of the new office, and Customs people were to be put in the most important executive posts.

The loss of professional direction and control in the Drug Enforcement Administration was dramatically manifested in a series of lawless raids on private homes in the Collinsville, Illinois, area in the spring of 1973. Joint Federal-local drug raids organized by members of the former Ambrose unit resulted in the entry of a number of private homes without search warrants, an assault on two persons, and the jailing of another for three days without filing charges. No illegal drugs were found during the entire episode.

All the careful work building morale and an effective Federal narcotics agency, to which Ingersoll had devoted years of effort, was now being destroyed. Ingersoll called a press conference to announce his resignation. He accused the Nixon Administration of fostering inter-agency rivalry, confusion, and White House intervention that had blunted effective narcotics enforcement. Ingersoll named H. R. Haldeman and John D. Ehrlichman as those White House aides who had attempted to thwart proper management of narcotics law enforcement. He said that the White House had gone beyond setting policy and tried to interfere directly with the way narcotics agencies went about their job. Ingersoll added that he had resisted such interference and said that was why he was being forced out of office. He pointed to the recent outrage of nighttime raids on the homes of innocent people in Illinois as examples of the kind of law enforcement standards the ODALE people were fostering. He condemned them unmercifully.

Ingersoll's warnings proved correct. The Drug Enforcement Administration limped along under divided leadership. By 1975, staff differences had broken out into open warfare. Washington newspaper columnist Jack Anderson published accusations of misconduct on the part of all of the top personnel in the agency, obviously leaked to him by some of the top men themselves. When the Senate Permanent Investigations Subcommittee scheduled hearings into the rapid decline in Federal narcotics law enforcement, Bartels was forced to resign. Reportedly he made a last-ditch effort to get Ambrose to intercede on his behalf, but Ambrose's connections at the White House were gone. But not completely forgotten. The undermining of Federal narcotics enforcement by the White House had done its work.

7

WHITE COLLARS
AND DIRTY HANDS

On a Sunday evening in May, 1969, Nathan Voloshen received a telephone call at his home in New York City from a man in California who identified himself as Delbert Coleman, chairman of Parvin/Dohrmann Company, the corporate owner of several Las Vegas casinos. Trading in Parvin/Dohrmann stock had just been halted by the SEC, which suspected irregularities in the way the company was conducting its business. Could Mr. Voloshen arrange for Mr. Coleman to meet with the chairman of the SEC? "Sure," came Voloshen's confident reply.

Two days later, Voloshen and Coleman were seated in the private office of Hamer Budge, chairman of the Securities and Exchange Commission, discussing how to straighten out Parvin/Dohrmann's troubles. Although Voloshen was never listed in SEC files as the attorney of record for Parvin/Dohrmann, he had important connections with John W. McCormack, then Speaker of the House of Representatives, and through the Speaker's office was able to arrange the appointment with the top man of the SEC on less than forty-eight hours' notice. For this service Voloshen received a fee of fifty thousand dollars.

Almost exactly three years later, Harry L. Sears, also not attorney of record, arranged for a private meeting with Hamer Budge's successor as chairman of the SEC, William J. Casey. The purpose of the meeting with Casey was to discuss the SEC's investigation of irregularities involving Robert Vesco and International Controls Corporation. This appointment was arranged on less than four hours' notice through former Attorney General John N. Mitchell. It came after Sears had delivered a $200,000 cash contribution on behalf of Vesco to the Committee for the Re-Election of the President. Mitchell was then chairman of CRP. Casey's successor in turn, G. Bradford Cook, continued to extend special courtesies to Sears and Vesco despite a major investigation into securities law violations currently being conducted by the SEC's staff.

Because of the lower-echelon integrity of the Commission's staff, the SEC investigations were not compromised, but the incidents point up some important facts about law enforcement practices in the white-collar field.

The most important is that three successive top officials of the nation's principal law enforcement agency in the securities industry have unhesitatingly welcomed people with good political connections who were trying to gain special consideration for suspected violators of securities laws. Moreover, until grand jury investigations were instituted in the Southern District of New York, no record or other evidence of any of the visits appeared in the Commission's official files.

The miraculous thing is that despite these lapses of judgment on the part of three successive SEC chairmen, the Commission staff has achieved an enviable record of enforcement against violations in the securities industry. This is largely due to the hardworking career staff in the Commission's enforcement arm, men like Irving M. Pollack and Stanley Sporkin, who have been unwavering in their commitment to evenhanded enforcement of the securities laws. Notwithstanding the use of political influence and cash to gain access to the SEC chairmen, Pollack,

Sporkin, and their colleagues were able to fend off outside pressures and enforce the law.

The courthouse phase of criminal securities cases is handled by the United States Attorneys. Over the years most of these cases have been brought in the Southern District of New York, where the Wall Street financial community is located. Because of the high volume of these cases, the Southern District office has established a special Frauds Unit to handle the investigation and prosecution of these complex cases, and has earned a well-deserved reputation for ability, hard work, and results.

The work of the U. S. Attorney's office in prosecuting white-collar crimes is not limited to securities law violations referred by the SEC. Securities cases tend to spawn other white-collar cases as witnesses and cooperating defendants are questioned by Assistant U. S. Attorneys. Frequently, those who are caught in one fraudulent scheme have also participated in others, and one investigative discovery usually leads to another. The strength of any U. S. Attorney's office working in white-collar law enforcement has been the development of experienced, knowledgeable Assistants who have learned how to investigate and try complex cases. This is one of the basic strengths of those U. S. Attorneys' offices that are able to attract a steady flow of bright young lawyers anxious for the chance to gain experience and to make a meaningful contribution to the community's ethical standards. It is also one of the cornerstones of Federal law enforcement.

THE ATTITUDE OF BUSINESS

On a hot July day in 1972, I made a speech to a Rotary Club at the Commodore Hotel in New York. I told the businessmen that the Federal prosecutor's office was receiving the least co-operation in combating crime from the business community. I warned them that if they did not come forward themselves with evidence of criminal conduct when it occurred, the U. S. Attorney's office would henceforth regard them as equally culpable unless their innocence was clearly established. Next morning, the remarks appeared on the front page of *The New York Times*.

George A. Spater, chairman of the board of American Airlines, read the story and conferred with the corporation's attorneys about information American had received indicating that an airline employee had accepted kickbacks from printing firms that handled promotional material. Mr. Spater instructed the company's attorneys to turn the matter over to our office. The Assistant U. S. Attorney in charge of the case initiated a grand jury investigation and discovered that there were several persons involved in the kickback scheme, including a corporate vice-president. Meanwhile, counsel for the airline started complaining about what they perceived as delay in prosecuting the dishonest employee. An indictment was returned in early February, 1973, charging two employees of American Airlines and the officers of a number of the printing firms in a commercial kickback and bribery scheme. When the indictment was filed and announced, the U. S. Attorney's office went out of its way to praise the action of American Airlines in bringing the facts to the attention of law enforcement officials:

> Although it risked potential adverse publicity, the company and its lawyers moved promptly and decisively to bring this violation to the attention of the proper prosecuting authorities. This positive attitude toward business ethics is in the highest traditions of the American enterprise system and deserves to be applauded and copied by other members of the business community.

American Airlines' public-relations office also issued a self-congratulatory response.

> American reaffirms its conviction that the best interests of the business community in such matters are served by

thoroughgoing cooperation with the appropriate government authorities.

Against this background, Federal officials were surprised to learn from the Watergate investigations that almost at the very time American's board chairman was instructing company counsel to report illegal conduct by a subordinate employee, the chairman was himself making illegal contributions to President Nixon's 1972 campaign. Spater admitted turning over a total of seventy-five thousand dollars *in cash,* of which all but twenty thousand dollars had come from corporate sources. The illegal contribution had been made in response to a solicitation by President Nixon's personal attorney, Herbert W. Kalmbach, who was then also counsel for United Airlines, American's major competitor. "I concluded that a substantial response was called for," Spater was quoted as commenting. It was noted that the airline had a proposed merger pending before the CAB at the time.

Too often business executives are hypocritical in their views about crime. They vigorously condemn muggers and robbers but silently tolerate their own kind of crime among colleagues. As a general rule, businessmen do *not* speak out against business crime. They do *not* condemn colleagues who cheat and lie and steal. They do *not* cooperate with law enforcement agencies. They do *not* express appreciation when law enforcement officials perform the job they should be doing themselves.

In a recent article in the *Wall Street Journal,* Professor Irving Kristol, of New York University, commented on complaints by businessmen that they were being unfairly criticized because of their pursuit of profits. Professor Kristol wrote that if the original idea behind capitalism had been only seeking profit and nothing more our form of free enterprise would never have come into existence—particularly in a civilization permeated by religious values and ideals. He noted capitalism's important moral dimensions, as evidenced by the popular Horatio Alger novels, which did not place major emphasis on the "profit motive." For Horatio Alger, the life of business was good because it helped to develop admirable traits of character: probity, diligence, thrift, self-reliance, self-respect, candor, fair dealing. Professor Kristol said that a deep moral decline has set into the business community as evidenced by the fact that its members now "placidly accept" the notion that their prime objective is profit.

From the standpoint of a prosecutor, there can be no doubt that the high level of white-collar crime is a direct result of the disappearance of moral values from the business community. Businessmen too easily accept the policy that any means that produce a profit are acceptable—whether the means involve bribing a public official, defrauding the Government, engaging in international financial frauds, or just plain cheating investors and customers. Where business leaders should combat unlawful conduct in their own community, Federal prosecutors have now had to take over the job by default.

THE IRVING CAPER

On January 9, 1972, billionaire recluse Howard Hughes spoke for three hours on a three-thousand-mile telephone connection from his retreat in the Bahama Islands. He was talking to seven journalists gathered in a Los Angeles hotel room. The reason for the press conference was Mr. Hughes's insistence that he had never authorized the "autobiography" by Clifford Irving that was about to be published jointly by McGraw-Hill and *Life* magazine. The book purported to consist of transcripts of taped conversations in various motels and parked cars between Hughes and Irving over a period of months. Hughes categorically denied ever having met the author, and denied the authenticity of his signature on canceled checks for the advances he had allegedly received from the publishers of the book.

Publishers Weekly, trade journal of the publishing world, reported that *Life* and McGraw-Hill still planned to go ahead with publication, and that they were convinced the autobiography was genuine.

> Life and McGraw-Hill said they had ample proof that the project was genuine, including a 10-page handwritten letter from Mr. Hughes to Harold W. McGraw, Jr., president of McGraw-Hill Book Company, and Mr. Hughes' signature on cancelled checks. The handwriting, the publishers said, had been verified by expert comparison of official documents bearing Mr. Hughes' signature. Finally, they say, they found the manuscript "completely convincing"—"no one who has read it can doubt its integrity, or, upon reading it, that of Clifford Irving."

Two months later, on March 13, 1972, Clifford Irving, together with his wife, Edith, and research assistant, Richard Suskind, pleaded guilty to charges of fraud, grand larceny, and related offenses arising from the greatest literary hoax in modern times. Irving was sentenced to two and one-half years' imprisonment; Suskind to six months; Edith Irving to two months. Subsequently, she was also sentenced to prison in Switzerland for committing a fraud on the Swiss banks.

Irving and Suskind had come up with the idea of concocting the fake autbiography at meetings on Majorca and on the Island of Ibiza in Spain. Irving had written a letter to Beverly Jane Loo, an editor at McGraw-Hill, stating that he had sent a copy of his novel *Fake!* to Howard Hughes and had received a warm response from him. A few weeks later, Irving sent a second letter to Ms. Loo advising that Hughes had expressed interest in having Irving write his autobiography. Then Irving forged three letters in the handwriting of Hughes, utilizing as a model a sample of Hughes's handwriting that had appeared in an issue of *Newsweek*. The forged letters expressed Hughes' desire to have Irving write his life story.

On February 10, 1971, Irving went to New York and met

with representatives of McGraw-Hill, showed them the three letters and began negotiations with the publishers to write the book. The author then went to Tehuantepec, Mexico, ostensibly for the purpose of meeting with Hughes. When he returned to New York, Irving told the McGraw-Hill people that he had met with Hughes twice in Mexico and that they had discussed contractual arrangements as well as material for the autobiography. During subsequent days, Irving worked out a letter agreement with the publisher which provided that the payments for the biography would be four hundred thousand dollars for Hughes and a hundred thousand for him. In early March, Irving went to San Juan, Puerto Rico, where he forged the signature of Hughes on the letter agreement and then returned to New York, where he displayed the forged agreement to the McGraw-Hill representatives. McGraw-Hill made the first payment on the advance and Irving executed a full publishing contract. He later expanded it to include publications of excerpts in *Life* magazine.

Irving and Suskind then set about collecting every piece of material on the eccentric billionaire they could lay their hands on. Suskind first went to the New York Public Library, then collected magazine articles and books from various secondhand book dealers. From New York, Suskind's quest took him to Las Vegas, Houston, and Los Angeles. Meanwhile, Irving went on to Washington, where he purloined from the Library of Congress a fifteen-hundred-page transcript of Hughes' 1947 testimony before a Senate subcommittee investigating war profiteering. He obtained other documents from the Atomic Energy Commission, the Civil Aeronautics Board, and the Defense Department. Then on to Miami, where he used a forged letter of introduction from a British publishing firm to try to obtain information about the Howard R. Hughes Medical Institute. Next stop was Paradise Island, in the Bahamas, where Irving continued to gather Hughes material, while letting McGraw-Hill believe that he was personally meeting with Hughes.

Irving had, in the meantime, altered a Swiss passport issued to his wife by the Swiss Consulate in Barcelona, Spain, by slightly changing the numbers and by renaming the passport holder "Helga R. Hughes." He affixed a photograph he had taken of his wife wearing a black wig and horn-rimmed glasses. Traveling with the forged passport, Mrs. Irving proceeded to Zurich, registered at a hotel and, wearing heavy makeup, a black wig, and the horn-rimmed glasses, opened an account in the name of H. R. Hughes at the Swiss Credit Bank. Forging the endorsement on a fifty-thousand-dollar check from Bankers Trust intended for the real "H. R. Hughes," Edith Irving deposited it in the Swiss Credit Bank. She then opened another account at a different bank, this time under the name Hanne Rosenkranz, and transferred some of the funds from the H. R. Hughes account into it. Later, she withdrew some of the funds in Swiss francs and took them back to her husband.

After obtaining additional research material from *Life*'s files, and stealing a draft biography by Noah Dietrich, Suskind and Irving returned to Ibiza and spent most of July and August, 1971, digesting the research material they had collected and conducting numerous tape-recorded interviews of each other, during which they would take turns assuming the role of Hughes. Except for bona fide material they had been able to obtain from the various sources they had visited, the interviews were completely fictionalized.

When the transcripts were typed and edited, Irving sent a telegram to Beverly Jane Loo at McGraw-Hill advising her that Hughes had demanded payment of a million dollars rather than the original half million agreed upon. He followed this with a letter saying that he had met with Hughes and spent the night persuading him to reduce his demand to $850,000. Irving and Suskind then went to Paradise Island, purportedly to meet with Hughes again, and then Irving went on to New York City, where he met with representatives of McGraw-Hill and *Life* and told them that during his meeting with Hughes on Paradise

Island he had given him copies of the 950-page transcript of interviews and that Hughes had annotated them with hand-written comments. The handwritten notes were in fact forgeries by Irving in Hughes' handwriting. A week later, Clifford Irving telephoned Beverly Jane Loo and told her that Hughes had agreed to reduce his demand further to $650,000.

On September 2, 1971, McGraw-Hill gave Clifford Irving a check in the amount of $275,000, payable to H. R. Hughes, which Irving agreed to deliver in person. The next day, Irving went to Key Biscayne, and sent a telegram back to McGraw-Hill reporting that he had personally delivered the check. Several days later, Edith Irving, wearing her black wig, went to Zurich and deposited the check in the H. R. Hughes account. The following month, wearing her same disguise, Mrs. Irving again returned to Zurich, and withdrew a large part of the funds from the H. R. Hughes account and transferred the sum to the Hanne Rosenkranz account, at the Swiss Banking Corporation.

On December 2, 1971, Irving again went to McGraw-Hill and picked up another check for H. R. Hughes, this time in the amount of $325,000, which he mailed off to the Swiss Credit Bank over the forged signature of H. R. Hughes.

On December 21, 1971, Irving delivered to McGraw-Hill the completed manuscript containing the fraudulent auto-biography of Howard Hughes. Hughes promptly repudiated the autobiography and instructed his lawyers to institute suit. Clifford Irving and Richard Suskind then executed sworn affidavits in opposition to a motion for an injunction, setting forth their entire false story in detail, this time under oath. A few weeks later, they publicly admitted their guilt.

How had it been possible to break the Irving case? Good investigative work, and luck. The official investigation got under way when Orison S. Marden, a senior partner in the law firm of White & Case, attorneys for McGraw-Hill, called on our office and the District Attorney. He advised us that after Hughes had repudiated the autobiography, his firm had conducted an investigation in Switzerland which had revealed that the account into which the payments to Howard Hughes had been deposited belonged not to Hughes but to a woman. That was the starting point.

Clifford Irving and his wife arrived in New York a few days later. They were summoned to the District Attorney's office, where they met with Leonard Newman, chief of the Frauds Bureau. Irving admitted to Newman that Helga R. Hughes was in fact his wife, Edith, but that was all. He claimed that she had handled the check transaction at the request of Hughes so that his associates would not be aware of what he was doing.

Meanwhile, Robert G. Morvillo, Chief of the Criminal Division in the U. S. Attorney's office, had asked the Post Office Inspection Service to conduct field investigations of the detailed factual claims made by Irving and Suskind as to the meetings with Hughes. District Attorney Frank Hogan and I met informally and agreed to exchange information and conduct the investigation jointly. The Post Office inspectors visited the various locations where Irving claimed to have met Hughes. They reviewed records of hotel stays and automobile rentals and other details of each visit. Slowly but surely, they pieced together proof that showed major discrepancies in Irving's story. Then they located Nina van Pallandt, with whom Clifford Irving had sojourned during his trip to Mexico, when he was supposedly meeting with Howard Hughes. Countess van Pallandt told the inspectors that Irving had spent all of his time with her. He had not been out of her sight long enough to meet with Howard Hughes or anyone else.

The investigative net began to close in on Irving. Morvillo had arranged to have a grand jury subpoena served on Irving's associate, Suskind, forcing his return to the United States and raising the possibility of his being a prosecution witness. Then, after Irving and his wife returned themselves, Morvillo obtained handwriting specimens from all of the principals and had them analyzed. The Post Office expert identified Irving's handwriting as having been done by the same person who forged the Hughes letters.

After that, the rest of the case centered on negotiations with Clifford Irving's chief counsel, Maurice Nessen, a former Assistant U. S. Attorney and a tough and effective lawyer. Morvillo and Nessen and other counsel in the case, including Assistant U. S. Attorney John J. Tigue, Jr., and Henry Putzel III, negotiated the conditions under which the Irvings and Suskind would agree to tell the truth.

The joint investigation between the Federal and local prosecutors worked out extremely well. The Federal investigators had access to Post Office inspectors, who could travel throughout the country and abroad, while the jurisdiction of the county office was limited to New York State. On the other hand, the county prosecutor had jurisdiction over a wide range of crimes, while the Federal office was limited in what it could prosecute.

As the publicity welled up around the Irving investigation, it became apparent that Irving was getting ready to profit again from his crime by offering to sell the rights to his story about the hoax. This would have been an injustice to the public and an affront to the administration of justice. Morvillo and his associates decided to do something about it. They prepared a long and detailed indictment that spelled out all of the essential facts right on the public record. Irving would not have a second chance to make a windfall out of his criminal scheme.

THE DUAL PERSONALITY OF THE IRS

Johnnie M. Walters was not a typical officeholder. A Southern gentleman, with sparkle, charm, and wit, he went about things differently from most public officials. When he wanted to get cooperation from a United States Attorney in moving tax fraud prosecutions or refund cases along, he did not call him on the telephone and bawl him out. Instead, he invited the man to Washington and took him off for a quiet picnic along the Potomac River, away from telephones and staff, where the two officials could talk face to face as friends and colleagues. Walters usually got what he wanted.

Early in the days of the Nixon Administration, Johnnie Walters was named Assistant Attorney General in charge of the Tax Division in the Department of Justice. Then, when Randolph Thrower resigned as Commissioner of Internal Revenue, Walters was moved into the post as head of IRS. The White House mistakenly believed that Walters would be "their man." They had a lot to learn.

Watergate conspirator John Caulfield prepared a memorandum for the White House on the need to make IRS more "politically responsive." In it he complained that the Administration had been "unable to stimulate audits of persons who should be audited." He also said that the White House had been unable "to obtain information in the possession of IRS regarding our political enemies." To remedy the situation the Caulfield memo said, the first step would be for Walters to make personnel changes so that IRS would be more "responsive" to the President. The second goal, wrote Caulfield, was to direct Walters to act on requests for political investigations.

> Walters should be told that discreet political action and investigations are a firm requirement and responsibility on his part. John Dean should have direct access to Walters, without Treasury clearance, for purposes of the White House. Walters should understand that when a request comes to him, it is his responsibility to accomplish it—without the White House having to tell him how to do it!

When White House Counsel John Dean turned over to Walters a list of 490 McGovern supporters with the request that IRS audit their tax returns, Walters quietly but firmly refused. He told Dean that to use the IRS for such a purpose would make the Watergate break-in look like "a Sunday-school picnic."

When Walters failed to go along with the Caulfield program he was eased out of government service.

Meanwhile, the White House had apparently found other ways to get help from the Internal Revenue Service. A number of audits of political "enemies" were arranged, and confidential information concerning audits of high political figures was turned over to the White House and leaked to the press. Dean told President Nixon during a taped conversation in the Oval Office on March 13, 1973, that he had developed other sources on the IRS staff and did not need Walters.

> *Nixon:* Do you need any IRS stuff?

> *Dean:* There is no need at this hour for anything from IRS, and we have a couple of sources over there that I can go to. I don't have to go around with Johnnie Walters or anybody, but we can get right in and get what we need.

Despite a handful of special audits and White House access to some confidential IRS information, there has not been any evidence of wholesale misuse of the Internal Revenue Service for political purposes. That is not altogether surprising. Earlier scandals involving political use of confidential tax returns produced very strict IRS security procedures. Access to tax information is rigidly controlled. Ironically, the problem at IRS is not loose procedures concerning private information about taxpayers. The problem is to get IRS to perform its basic job of investigating and prosecuting tax violators with any degree of vigor.

The potential of Federal tax prosecutions as an effective weapon against corruption and white-collar crime is immense. Tax prosecutions have already proved of major importance against gangsters, organized crime figures, and major narcotics dealers. Going back to the time of Al Capone, Frank Costello, and, more recently, the Department of Justice Strike Forces' investigations of organized crime figures, the tax investigation and prosecution powers have brought to justice many law violators who otherwise would have escaped prosecution entirely. The reason is simple: anyone who earns income is obligated to file a tax return. If he is engaged in illegal activity, the chances are he will not tell the truth on his return, or he will fail to pay full taxes on his illegal profits. All forms of illegal activity—bribery, securities fraud, embezzlement, and many other variations—produce income that is taxable and must be reported. When that income is concealed, a Federal criminal violation has taken place.

On the lower echelons, the IRS is quite well equipped to do first-rate law enforcement work. Many IRS offices display high morale and top investigative talent. Accountants and field agents who have had the satisfaction of winning convictions against law violators have a special feel for the job. With several years' experience they develop a "sixth sense" as to where concealed income is likely to show up. They know how to go through a pile of canceled checks and spot the ones that are not in the usual pattern, which often lead to some form of fraud. In the Frank Costello income-tax prosecution, for example, a five-dollar canceled check to a florist first put IRS agents on a trail that led them to a family mausoleum for which Costello had paid many thousands of dollars, all in cash. The amount of that expenditure, plus the way it was paid, proved to be an important element of proof in the net-worth tax case on which Costello was later convicted.

Concern about unauthorized disclosure of taxpayer information, combined with a past pattern of corruption in fixing tax cases, has produced IRS administrative regulations and procedures that would try the patience of anyone. The most chronic problem concerns the delay in criminal tax cases. Once a special agent has completed his final report on an investigation and recommended prosecution, that report starts a long, tortuous trip through the regional office of the IRS, the national office of the IRS, the Tax Division of the Department of Justice, and then to the United States Attorney's office. The IRS district office where the case begins and the U. S. courthouse where it will be prosecuted are often only a few blocks apart. Yet it is not unusual for a criminal tax case to take two years to travel the distance from one office to the other, by way of Washington. This long delay is unfair to the defendant, unfair to the public, and unfair to the law enforcement personnel who invest so much effort in the case. Over such a long period of time, memories grow dim, witnesses die or disappear, and the enthusiasm of the special agent is lost, as he turns his attention to new cases during the intervening period.

One particularly bad symptom of the delay problem is the Tax Division's practice of referring tax cases to U. S. Attorneys for prosecution just a few days before the six-year statute of limitations expires. This leaves the Assistant U. S. Attorneys virtually no time for review of the strengths and weaknesses of the case and the possible need for additional investigation. The facts of the case are by then stale and all but forgotten, and the events are so distant that it is hard for a sentencing judge to regard the violation very seriously.

A related problem in the processing of criminal tax cases is the total isolation of the investigating agent from the prosecutor's office until after the investigation of the case has been completed. This means that when a special agent needs help in obtaining information or documents from a third-party witness he cannot request the aid of the U. S. Attorney in issuing a grand jury subpoena and opening up a grand jury investigation that will ultimately result in an indictment. Instead, the special agent has to rely on an administrative-summons procedure, which is drawn out and usually completely ineffective if the third party persists in his refusal to turn over information. What a grand jury subpoena can achieve in a matter of days the IRS special agent can accomplish often only after months of delay, if then. There are other IRS regulations that compound the problem, such as the prohibition against IRS agents working jointly with Assistant U. S. Attorneys in reviewing exhibits and testimony in grand jury investigations for possible tax violations. All of these difficulties are well known to Federal investigators and prosecutors, but the administrative hierarchies in both IRS and the Tax Division of the Justice Department stubbornly refuse to budge. The public pays the price.

8

MONEY CORRUPTS
ABSOLUTELY

On November 24, 1970, Robert T. Carson, assistant to U. S. Senator Hiram Fong, of Hawaii, met with Deputy Attorney General Richard G. Kleindienst in the latter's office at the Department of Justice. The two men were alone. After exchanging pleasantries, Carson sat down in a chair in front of Kleindienst's desk. He told the Justice official that he had a friend in New York who was in trouble. He said that if Kleindienst could help his friend he would make a contribution of between fifty and a hundred thousand dollars to the reelection of President Nixon.

"Helping," it turned out, meant doing something to stop a criminal prosecution for securities fraud which was then pending in the Southern District of New York. Mr. Kleindienst politely refused and changed the subject.

A week later, Attorney General Mitchell showed Kleindienst an FBI memorandum reporting that the U. S. Attorney in New York had initiated an investigation and that an undercover agent wearing a concealed tape recorder was having conversations in Senator Fong's office concerning an attempt to fix a securities fraud case through the Deputy Attorney General's

office. Kleindienst immediately sat down and dictated a memorandum for the files reporting his conversation with Carson the
week before.

Kleindienst was later called as a Government witness in the
criminal-bribery trial of Carson in the Southern District of New
York. He related his earlier conversation concerning the bribe
offer from Carson during his direct testimony. Then he was
asked by Carson's lawyer, on cross-examination, why he had not
said or done anything about the conversation until a week afterward. Kleindienst's answer startled everyone in the courtroom.

> Q. It is true, then, is it not, that on November 24,
> 1970, you did not regard that in the conversation you
> had with Mr. Carson that he offered you a bribe?
>
> A. No, I did not.

The jury, however, had no trouble recognizing the bribe
offer, and brought in a verdict of guilty against Carson, for
which he subsequently went to prison. The incident dramatizes
the importance of independent United States Attorneys' offices
in maintaining the integrity of Federal law enforcement.

SPIRO AGNEW AND COMPANY

Spiro Agnew could not understand what all the hubbub was
about. He declared, "I at no time conducted my official duties
as County Executive or Governor of Maryland in a manner
harmful to the interests of the county or state, or my duties
as Vice-President of the United States in a manner harmful to
the nation. My acceptance of contributions was part of a long-
established pattern of political fund-raising in the state. At no
time have I enriched myself at the expense of the public trust."

Agnew was responding to a forty-page summary of evidence
and criminal information charging him with income-tax evasion. The evidence against him had been submitted to the U. S.

District Court in Maryland, where, on October 10, 1973, he entered a plea of *nolo contendere,* or no contest, against the charges.

A few days later, the former Vice-President was allowed a last hurrah in a final appearance on network television. Agnew took advantage of the occasion to reassert his innocence and to blame the prosecution against him on a new, "post-Watergate morality."

Agnew, brought up in the traditions of local Maryland politics, had become immersed in patterns of payoffs and corruption. He openly told those who solicited kickbacks for him that he needed additional cash to cope with the added expenses of his higher political station in life. He purchased a $190,000 home in 1973, with a $160,000 mortgage, and blithely told friends that he could not afford to buy new draperies. A close associate later described Agnew as a man who felt that he had to maintain the appearances of his high office. Since he was not a man of personal wealth, it was only right that those who benefited by his position should help pay the cost.

Particularly ironic was the fact that the most damaging testimony against Agnew had come from his staunchest political supporter, I. H. Hammerman II. Hammerman was a successful real-estate developer and mortgage banker, who at the time of the grand jury investigation had already launched an Agnew-for-President movement and had helped finance the distribution of bumper stickers touting "Spiro of '76." "Bud" Hammerman had pledged to raise several million dollars for Agnew's 1976 presidential bid before he became the last, and the most important, of the four central witnesses who brought about Agnew's fall.

The other three witnesses who provided the evidence of bribery were engineers engaged in obtaining government contracts. One was Allen Green, president and one of the principal owners of Green Associates, Inc., a Maryland engineering company. The second was Lester Matz, president of Matz, Childs and

Associates, Inc., and an engineer operating in Maryland for approximately twenty-four years. The third was Jerome B. Wolff, president of Greiner Environmental Systems, Inc., who had been Assistant Director of Public Works for Baltimore County when Agnew first became a member of the Board of Zoning Appeals, and who later followed Agnew into the Governor's office as chairman of the State Roads Commission.

Details of the payoffs to Agnew from his earliest days as County Executive of Baltimore County were set forth in sworn statements filed with the United States Attorney during the course of the investigation that resulted in Agnew's indictment and resignation.

Allen Green told the prosecutors that he had been an engineer in Maryland for twenty-one years and that during this period he had often made payments on behalf of his company in return for state and local consulting contracts. These payments were always made in cash so that they could not be traced. The payments reflected his understanding of a system under which a firm such as his had to make payoffs to insure its survival and growth. Green said that the system had developed long ago in Maryland and existed in other states as well. Under Maryland procedures, engineering contracts are not awarded on the basis of public bids. Instead, the selection of engineers for state-road contracts has rested exclusively in the discretion of the members of the State Roads Commission and the Governor himself. There are many engineering companies that seek state contracts, and engineers are therefore extremely vulnerable to pressure from officials for under-the-table payments. An engineer who refuses to pay has no effective recourse when he fails to receive public work, while those who do make payments can safely expect that they will be appropriately rewarded.

Some of the major engineering companies reach the point of such expertise that their services are essential to state construction jobs. They therefore no longer have to make cash payments in order to receive business. It is the smaller firms that are particularly susceptible to requests for illegal payments, because of the ease with which work can be given to others. As each new state administration came into office, it inherited a tacit understanding that engineers would make kickback payments if they expected to receive public work. When a politician requested a payment or an engineer offered one it was not necessary for anyone to specify the purposes. Everyone knew what was expected.

Allen Green first met Spiro Agnew when he was County Executive for Baltimore County, and cultivated his relationship by occasionally having lunch with Agnew. When Spiro Agnew ran for Governor, in 1966, Green was one of his substantial campaign contributors. He contributed in part because he genuinely admired the man and believed that he would make a good Governor, but also because he expected Agnew to be grateful. Green anticipated that Agnew's gratitude would be expressed in terms of state contracts.

After his inauguration as Governor, Agnew met with Green on several occasions in his new office. At one of these meetings Agnew expressed his concern about the substantial financial obligations imposed upon him by his new position. He told Green, according to the statement filed in court by the U. S. Attorney, that as titular head of the Republican Party in Maryland he would need substantial funds to support his own political organization. In addition, Agnew believed that he would be called upon to provide financial assistance to other Republican candidates around the state. He also complained that it was extremely difficult for a person in his limited financial situation to bear the personal expenses of high public office, since his new position required him to maintain a life-style that was beyond his means. He said that he had served as County Executive at a substantial financial sacrifice and that the increase in salary as Governor was still insufficient to meet the additional demands his new position imposed upon him.

The implications of Agnew's remarks were not lost on Green. He immediately responded that his company had experienced successful growth and would probably continue to benefit from public work under the Agnew Administration. Therefore, he would be pleased to make periodic cash payments to the Governor. Agnew responded that such assistance would be very much appreciated.

Green calculated that his firm could afford to pay an average of 1 percent of fees on public engineering contracts and still make a comfortable profit. He therefore arranged to meet with the Governor approximately six times a year and on each occasion handed the Governor personally an envelope containing between two and three thousand dollars in currency. On each occasion, Green referred to the Governor's financial needs and his desire to be of assistance. Agnew usually placed the envelope containing the cash in his desk drawer or in his coat pocket. In time, less and less was said about the reason for the payment, and Green would simply hand over the envelope during the course of idle conversation. He would not let the occasion pass, however, without making some reference to state-road contracts, frequently referring to specific future contracts on which his company hoped to receive consideration. Occasionally, Agnew would promise that Green's company would receive specific contracts, or would tell him that a contract had already been committed to another company. There was no doubt in Green's mind that the principal purpose for making payments to Governor Agnew was to influence him to select Green's company for as many state-road contracts as possible. Green firmly believed that such payments were necessary in the light of past experience and would certainly be helpful in guaranteeing a continued flow of state work.

Allen Green paid Governor Agnew over twenty thousand dollars during the two years Agnew served as Governor of Maryland, obtaining the cash through devious methods concealed in the company's books. Occasionally he was asked by the chairman of the State Roads Commission whether he was taking care of "his obligations" with respect to the substantial state work that he had been receiving. Green said he was.

Following Agnew's election as Vice-President in 1968, Jerome B. Wolff, chairman of the Maryland State Roads Commission, met with Green. Wolff showed him a list of contracts Green's firm had received from the State Roads Commission under the Agnew administration. The two men discussed the contracts and fees and the extent to which the work could be attributed to contracts awarded during the preceding administration. Ultimately they reached agreement on a list of state work that Green believed was due to Agnew's administration. The total fees on these contracts amounted to between three and four million dollars. One percent came to between thirty and forty thousand dollars. Green met with the Vice-President-elect in his Baltimore office and delivered another regular payment.

Agnew began this first post-election conversation with Green by referring to the same list of contracts that Green's company had received, noting that there had been a lot of work from the State Roads Commission and that he, Agnew, was glad that things had worked out that way. He then returned to a familiar theme: he had not improved his personal financial situation during his two years as Governor and, although he would now receive an even higher salary as Vice-President, he anticipated that the demands of the office would substantially increase his personal expenses. For these reasons, he said, he hoped that Green would be able to continue the financial assistance that he had been providing over the preceding two years and the Vice-President, in turn, believed he could be helpful to Green in connection with Federal contracts. Green agreed to the request.

After Agnew became Vice-President, Green called on Agnew three or four times a year, either in his office, in the Executive Building in Washington, or in his apartment, at the Park Sheraton Hotel, and handed him envelopes containing two thousand dollars in cash. The two men were always alone when the payments were made. The last payment occurred in December, 1972. Green got wind of the Federal investigation shortly thereafter and stopped making payments.

Over the six years between 1966 and 1972, Green's payments of cash to Spiro T. Agnew had totaled approximately fifty thousand dollars.

Lester Matz told the prosecutors essentially the same story of payoffs during Agnew's administration as Governor. After Agnew was elected Vice-President, Matz placed ten thousand dollars in cash in an envelope. He went to Washington and met privately with Agnew in the Vice-President's office and showed him a paper on which he had calculated what he owed on state contracts. Matz then turned over the envelope, which Agnew casually placed in his desk drawer. The two men agreed that whenever Matz was ready to make further payments to the Vice-President he would telephone Agnew's secretary and tell her that he had more "information" for the Vice-President.

Some time later, in 1970 or early 1971, the Agnew associate to whom Matz had earlier made payments when Agnew was County Executive telephoned him to say that there was a Federal project coming up on which the Vice-President could control the engineering contracts. Matz was informed that he could receive a contract on the "usual" terms. Matz asked that the contract be awarded to a company in which he and his partner had an interest, and this was done. Matz then made an appointment to meet with the Vice-President and delivered to him an envelope containing twenty-five hundred dollars in currency as the kickback on the Federal contract.

The following spring, the Agnew associate pressured Matz to make a substantial contribution to the 1972 Nixon-Agnew campaign. Matz refused and later complained about the solicitation to the Vice-President. Agnew replied with a smile, "Tell him you gave at the office."

The third engineer who became a witness in the Agnew investigation, Jerome B. Wolff, told the prosecutors that he got to know Spiro Agnew when the latter first became a member of the Baltimore County Board of Zoning Appeals, in the late nineteen-fifties, and Wolff appeared regularly as a witness before the board. Wolff left government employment shortly after Agnew took office as County Executive, but he and Agnew became good friends while he operated as a consulting engineer. Wolff served as a sort of unofficial adviser to Agnew, and the County Executive, in return, arranged for him to receive county engineering contracts. Wolff admired Agnew and believed that he was sincerely trying to do a good job. During this period, Wolff was occasionally called upon to make modest payments to various Agnew associates when he received county contracts, and he was aware that other engineering firms were also making payments in order to get public work.

When Agnew ran for Governor of Maryland, in 1966, Wolff made a thousand-dollar cash contribution, which he handed to the candidate personally. He also worked as a volunteer in Agnew's campaign and was aware that Agnew might appoint him to public office if he were elected. The expectations were fulfilled when Governor Agnew named Jerome Wolff chairman of the Maryland State Roads Commission, in March, 1967. Wolff's job was to monitor every consulting, engineering, and construction contract that came through the state, thereby maintaining control over the selection of all engineers and architects on state-road contracts, subject only to ultimate review by the Governor himself.

At this point, "Bud" Hammerman entered the picture.

Wolff had known Hammerman as a real-estate developer when Wolff was Assistant Director of Public Works in Baltimore. After he went into private practice, he did most of the engineering work on Hammerman's construction projects. Hammerman had also become acquainted with Spiro Agnew during this period. Although he had supported Agnew's opponent for County Executive in 1962, Hammerman had mended his fences quickly by offering to make a contribution toward Agnew's campaign deficit. Agnew told him that he would prefer a contribution of three times the amount when he ran for office again. The two men developed a close personal relationship, and they often discussed Agnew's personal financial situation. Agnew told Hammerman that he had not accumulated any wealth before he assumed public office, had no inheritance, and received only a small salary as a public official. Not only did his public position require him to adopt a standard of living beyond his means, but his future ambitions required him to build a financially strong political organization. Hammerman offered to help. He made substantial personal gifts to Agnew, entertained him frequently, and introduced him to potential campaign contributors.

When Agnew ran for Governor, in 1966, Hammerman became one of Agnew's financial chairmen, even though most of his business associates were supporting the opposition, Democratic candidate. He personally contributed twenty-five thousand dollars to the Agnew campaign and raised substantially more in campaign gifts from others. Hammerman's relationship with Agnew continued, and he regularly entertained and traveled with the future Vice-President, providing him with financial assistance.

Shortly after Agnew became Governor of Maryland, he had a conversation with Hammerman in his official office in Annapolis. The new Governor explained that there was a long-standing "system" under which engineers made substantial cash contributions in return for the award of state contracts through the State Roads Commission. Agnew requested Hammerman to help him collect cash payments from the engineers and instructed him to meet with Jerome Wolff to work out the details. Thereafter, the three men entered into an arrangement under which Wolff would award the contracts, Hammerman would collect the payments, and the Governor would receive most of the proceeds. The cash was divided 50 percent to Agnew, and 25 percent each to Hammerman and Wolff.

The arrangement worked smoothly throughout Agnew's term as Governor of Maryland. The engineers in Maryland quickly learned that Hammerman was the man to see when they wanted state jobs. When Wolff awarded contracts to these engineers, he would alert Hammerman, who would then telephone the successful firm and offer his congratulations. This was the signal that a "contribution" was expected, and they were always forthcoming—and always in cash. Hammerman placed Agnew's share of the payoffs in a safe-deposit box and held it until it was requested by the Governor. From time to time Agnew would telephone Hammerman and ask him how many "papers" Hammerman had. By prior agreement the word "paper" meant a thousand dollars. When Hammerman told Agnew he had thirty papers, it mean thirty thousand dollars in cash in the safe-deposit box. Agnew would then tell him how many "papers" to bring to him, and Hammerman would remove the money from the safe-deposit box and personally deliver it to Agnew. Under the Agnew-Hammerman-Wolff arrangement, Hammerman regularly collected cash payments from seven different engineering firms in return for state engineering contracts, and also from one financial institution in return for an award to finance state bonds. Both Hammerman and Wolff were aware that Lester Matz and Allen Green were making payments directly to the Governor.

There came a time when this arrangement was jeopardized. Hammerman had been especially heavy-handed in trying to solicit payments from one particular engineer, who had resisted. The engineer complained to his attorney, who happened to be a close personal friend of Agnew's. The attorney met with Agnew and gave him a detailed account of Hammerman's solicitation and warned him that Hammerman could undermine all that Governor Agnew was attempting to accomplish. Agnew promised to look into the matter, but the attorney never heard anything further. Several months later, he insisted that Agnew meet with his client, the engineer, which the Governor did. But nothing changed; Agnew continued to operate as before.

When Spiro T. Agnew submitted his resignation as Vice-President and entered his plea of *nolo contendere* in the United States District Court in Baltimore, he explicitly denied that he had been influenced in the conduct of his official duties. He did admit receiving payments during 1967 which were not expended for political purposes and that those payments were therefore income taxable to him. He also admitted that contracts had been awarded by state agencies to the firms on whose behalf such payments had been made and that he was aware of the awards. He stressed that "no contracts were awarded to contractors who were not competent to perform the work." And he maintained that he at no time conducted his official duties in a manner harmful to the interests of the people. Except for not paying his taxes, he still would not admit that what he had done was wrong.

GEORGE BEALL AND COMPANY

The Agnew prosecution and conviction were triumphs for the office of the United States Attorney in Baltimore, and portrayed the workings of a Federal prosecutor's office at its best. The case underscored the value of talent, enthusiasm, and hard work by a team of idealistic young lawyers. But it also represented the quality of commitment and effort in many U.S. Attorneys' offices throughout the country. The key ingredients are dedicated staff, creativity in approach, and absolute independence and integrity.

The Agnew investigation had begun over a luncheon table in a Baltimore restaurant a year and a half earlier. Seated at the table, deep in conversation, were the IRS intelligence chief in Maryland, Robert Browne, and United States Attorney George Beall. The time was March, 1972. Browne and Beall had worked together on a number of cases and had become friends. They were discussing what they should be doing as Federal law enforcement officials in view of the rumors about payoffs and kickbacks in the Baltimore County government. Browne volunteered to do some digging.

The IRS official quietly dispatched a team of special agents to plow through the records of companies that had been doing regular business with the county. By October, Browne reported to Beall that his agents had found evidence that a number of engineering and architectural firms had been generating large sums of unexplained cash. To any law enforcement man, unexplained cash always raises the possibility of corruption. Beall assigned two young Assistant United States Attorneys to work on the investigation. Two months later, they recommended the convening of a special grand jury.

Beall and his two Assistants then paid a call on Herbert Stern, U. S. Attorney for New Jersey, whose office had a brilliant track record in exposing corruption in municipal government. Stern, articulate and enthusiastic, told the Baltimore prosecutors the basic lessons his staff had learned. The first rule, he said, was "Look for pools of cash." He suggested that the prosecutors subpoena company books and records and search for phony invoices, checks, and other devices used for the concealment of cash payments. Proof of concealment would provide leverage to persuade company officials to talk. The Maryland team headed home to put the Stern formula to work. They blanketed Baltimore with subpoenas while IRS agents screened documents. Before they were through, the U. S. Attorney's office had accumulated 120 filing cabinets full of papers. The task was enormous.

The records of one architectural firm contained a number of canceled checks reflecting loans to corporate officers. When the IRS agents examined the checks themselves, they found that they had all been endorsed for cash. The firm's executives were brought in for questioning. They gave the first glimpse of the pattern of corruption which had existed in Baltimore County for years. These particular payments had been made to William Fornoff, purportedly a go-between for higher officials.

The testimony from the architects had been a lucky break, but it was short-lived. Thereafter the investigation ran into a stone wall. Other executives were not so willing to talk. The prosecutors were forced to go at the investigation by an even more circuitous route, by calling in scores of employees for questioning. Slowly but surely, they worked up the ladder, using immunity and persuasion. In June, 1973, Fornoff was indicted. He immediately entered a plea of guilty. Guilt-conscious observers jumped to the conclusion that Fornoff had agreed to cooperate with the Government and was undoubtedly providing evidence against them. Attorneys for Lester Matz and Jerome Wolff made appointments to meet with the Assistant U. S. Attorneys. They wanted to explore the possibility of working out a deal for their clients, too.

Matz provided the first evidence that payments had been made directly to Agnew. Then Wolff told the prosecutors about the three-way split between Agnew, Hammerman, and himself. Green came in next, and started telling about his payments to Agnew.

U. S. Attorney Beall delivered a letter to Judah Best, attorney for Agnew, advising him that his client was under investigation for tax evasion, bribery, and extortion. The letter found its way into the *Wall Street Journal*. It was not long before I. H. Hammerman came to the courthouse to try to work out the best deal he could. The rest is history.

Agnew's lawyers drove a hard bargain. They wanted a guarantee of no prison term in return for his immediate resignation from office. If they did not get that commitment, they said, they were going to fight the case all the way. Agnew backed up these statements by making speeches attacking the prosecution and the prosecution's witnesses. He publicly asked Congress to investigate his conduct. He challenged the jurisdiction of the district court to prosecute him without prior impeachment by Congress. Agnew's lawyers launched a counteroffensive. They obtained a court order authorizing subpoenas to inquire into the source of press leaks about the investigation—the one black mark that had marred the whole episode.

The Baltimore U. S. Attorney's staff was incensed that Agnew was using his position as first in line of succession to the Presidency as a ploy to avoid going to jail. Attorney General Richardson was more practical. The nation would suffer badly if there was a prolonged legal proceeding when it was always possible that something might happen to the President (as it later did) and a corrupt Vice-President would take over the Government. Richardson told George Beall and his colleagues that he personally would assume responsibility for recommending the acceptance of a *nolo* plea and no prison term. That was enough to persuade the U. S. Attorney's staff that the Attorney General was a "stand-up guy," and they agreed on condition that a detailed summary of the evidence would also be filed so that no one could ever say there had been a cover-up.

Many people have been critical of the "deal" by which a major white-collar criminal got off without a prison sentence, but no thoughtful person can doubt that Attorney General Richardson acted in good faith and did what he believed was in the national interest. The fault lay with Agnew's use of his position to blackmail the prosecution into agreeing to almost anything in order to get him out of office as quickly as possible.

The most troublesome aspect of the Agnew case, apart from the national tragedy it represented, was that the case illustrated typical dealings between businessmen and government officials. Payoffs and kickbacks were accepted as routine. Unfortunately, that attitude is widespread. When confronted with a solicitation or offer of a bribe, few officials or businessmen react with

167

outrage or surprise. Instead, the transaction is usually completed as if it were an everyday matter. Happily, there are still a few who resist such practices—such as the lone engineer in Baltimore who complained about Hammerman's solicitation of kickbacks on state contracts. Until the business community does something to change its own ethics, and the ethics of the officials it supports for public office, the task of combating corruption and perversion of government will fall on U. S. Attorneys and their staffs.

What was unusual about the Agnew prosecution from a law enforcement point of view was not that the Vice-President was corrupt, shocking as that fact was, but that the Federal prosecution team was able to assemble the necessary proof in the face of IRS restrictions and Department of Justice red tape. IRS agents became investigators for the grand jury; they served grand jury subpoenas; they worked side by side with Assistant U. S. Attorneys in reviewing records and witness testimony; and they investigated a wide range of Federal crimes in addition to tax violations. The results spoke for themselves.

Knowing the obstacles IRS usually presents to broad-ranging investigations, I wrote to George Beall a few months after the Agnew conviction to ask how he had achieved such good cooperation. He acknowledged that when the Washington bureaucrats woke up to what had happened in the Agnew case the process of strangulation had set in again.

> I am only now beginning to realize how lucky I was in having the kind of Chief of Intelligence that I did. Since our Agnew experience, retrenchment seems to be the prevailing attitude in Washington at the Department and at IRS. Since last fall I have been told IRS has been issuing internal orders to revenue and special agents which have the accumulative effect of reducing their participation in investigative projects directed at local political corruption.
>
> Justice, too, has begun to raise obstacles to these kinds

of investigations by pulling out technical interpretations from the U. S. Attorney's Manual as to use of statutes like the Hobbs Act, like 26 U.S.C. 7212 and like the use immunity provision of the 18 U.S.C. 6001.

As the Agnew case dramatically demonstrated, IRS investigators have the capacity to perform extraordinarily well in combating official corruption and white-collar crime in concert with local U. S. Attorneys. The problem is that middle-management personnel in IRS and the Department of Justice seem bent on doing everything they can to throw roadblocks in the way. This is not a matter of political abuse by an insensitive President or amoral Attorney General. It is part of the existing career establishment of Federal law enforcement.

ENTER ORGANIZED CRIME

Two weeks after the indictment and conviction of Spiro Agnew, in Baltimore, a Federal grand jury in New York City filed an indictment against Brooklyn Congressman Frank J. Brasco, charging him with conspiracy to receive $27,500 in illegal payoffs in 1968 from a Bronx trucking concern in connection with Federal contracts to haul the U. S. mails. The indictment alleged that the Congressman interceded with the Post Office to obtain a truck-leasing contract for the A.N.R. Leasing Corporation, even though six other firms had submitted lower bids. Thereafter, Representative Brasco attempted to obtain an $875,000 loan for the corporation to help it finance the purchase of trucks to perform the contract.

The striking difference between the Brasco indictment and the Agnew prosecution was that the man from whom the Congressman had agreed to accept the bribes was not just another businessman. He was John Masiello, a "captain" in the organized crime family of the late Vito Genovese, and reportedly a major figure in Mafia rackets in Westchester County before he went to prison, in 1970. This was not Masiello's first involvement in bribing public officials. In March, 1970, he was sentenced to five years in prison for paying bribes to Post Office officials to ignore complaints about a trucking company he controlled. In 1971, Masiello was again convicted in Federal court for bribing an IRS agent to obtain information about a pending tax investigation. Edward M. Shaw, the Assistant United States Attorney who had first convicted Masiello and who was later put in charge of the Organized Crime Strike Force in New York, had persuaded Masiello to cooperate with the Government. He thus became the highest-ranking member of the crime syndicate ever to provide testimony for a government agency in a criminal case. The result was particularly auspicious, because the first investigation of Brasco, by the U. S. Attorney's office in Baltimore, had been terminated in 1971 because of insufficient evidence. Masiello changed all that by agreeing to testify. He said that he had personally delivered ten thousand dollars in cash to Congressman Brasco in his Capitol Hill office. Brasco was subsequently convicted and sentenced to jail.

Corruption of public officials is one of the standard techniques of organized crime. The practice is doubly sinister because it facilitates the unlawful operations from which the Mafia gains most of its funds. The principal source of cash for organized-crime operations comes from gambling. The "numbers game," bookmaking, and bets on sporting events provide the lion's share of dollars for organized crime families. The second principal source of funds is loan-sharking. Besides providing a lucrative source of funds, gambling debts and loan-shark payments also provide opening wedges into legitimate business. Other big money-makers in organized crime activity are labor racketeering, hijacking, and pornography. The most destructive project of organized crime families has been the distribution of narcotics.

Some of the businesses in which Federal investigators have discovered Mafia penetration are trucking, garment-making, meat-packing, private cartage, pizza parlors, bars and restaurants, funeral homes, real estate, construction, catering, retailing, jewelry, and beverage-bottling. Organized crime participation has also been found occasionally in electronics firms, artificial-flower manufacturers, dry-cleaning establishments, auto-body and fender-repair concerns, ice-cream manufacturers, fruit-handlers, vending-machine companies, fish wholesalers, service stations, scrap-metal dealers, roofing firms, pet shops, and plumbing contractors. In short, there are very few fields in which organized crime has not found entry, usually using funds obtained from illegal sources with the help of corrupt public officials.

The recent conviction of major organized crime figures in securities fraud cases is a tribute to effective Federal law enforcement, but it is also symptomatic of the increasing participation of organized crime in complex business operations.

The evils that flow from infiltration of local government by organized crime were highlighted by the extraordinary series of prosecutions initiated by the U. S. Attorney's office in New Jersey under Frederick Lacey and Herbert Stern. During the early nineteen-seventies, a number of high public officials in state and local government were convicted in Federal court and sent to prison: Hugh J. Addonizio, former Mayor of Newark; Thomas Whalen, former Mayor of Jersey City; Richard Jackson, former Mayor of Atlantic City; William T. Sommers, his successor as Mayor of Atlantic City; Robert Burkhardt, former Secretary of State of the State of New Jersey; Paul Sherwin, Burkhardt's successor as Secretary of State; John A. Kervick, former State Treasurer; Fred Kropke, former Chief of Police of Hudson. This extraordinary parade of public officeholders was a sorry spectacle that briefly shocked most Americans. Unfortunately, without more lasting changes in attitude, there can be no assurance that these same practices will not continue, only in more sophisticated forms that will become harder to detect.

CAN CORRUPTION BE STOPPED?

In 1973, a three-judge panel of the U. S. Court of Appeals for the Second Circuit reversed the conviction of an assistant district attorney charged with accepting a bribe to fix a state-court indictment. The appellate court dismissed the case on the ground that there was no Federal jurisdiction. But the judges did not stop there. They went out of their way to criticize the investigative technique that had been used to develop the case against the corrupt state prosecutor. That technique had involved an extremely able undercover Federal agent, Sante Bario, who let himself be arrested in Queens County for possession of a loaded pistol. The agent had then gone to a reportedly corrupt bail bondsman, who steered him in turn to a leading local criminal lawyer. The lawyer said he could have the case fixed for fifteen thousand dollars. When the lawyer told the undercover agent that the other party to the arrangement was the chief of the indictment bureau of the Queens County District Attorney's office, responsible for processing more than four thousand felony cases a year, it became apparent that the D. A.'s office was deeply infected by corruption and that something had to be done.

Following orders from the U. S. Attorney's office, the undercover agent delivered fifteen thousand dollars in marked bills to the corrupt lawyer and carried out his instructions to appear before the grand jury. As promised, the grand jury did not indict the agent. Shortly thereafter a search warrant was executed on the assistant district attorney's home, and investigators turned up several of the marked bills. Here was proof of the worst kind of corruption of the administration of criminal justice.

Now the Federal court of appeals was admonishing the Federal prosecutor for permitting the undercover agent to play the role of an underworld gunman and for testifying falsely before the grand jury in compliance with the defendant's instructions.

> While this pattern of deception may be less serious than some forms of governmental participation in crime that can be hypothesized, it is substantially *more offensive* [italics added] than the common cases where government agents induce the sale of narcotics in order to make drug arrests.

To whom was it "more offensive"? Had the fact that judges and assistant district attorneys were now the targets of Federal investigation, rather than narcotics dealers, changed the rules? That is the way it looked to the outside world.

The appeals court decision caused an uproar in the law enforcement community. District Attorney Frank S. Hogan filed an *amicus curiae* brief strongly urging that the court's dictum disapproving the investigative technique should be "disavowed." Another *amicus* brief was filed on behalf of Maurice Nadjari, the new Special Prosecutor who had recently been appointed to look into corruption in the criminal justice system. Nadjari said that the undercover operations conducted by the U. S. Attorney's office were a "reasonable, imaginative, and effective law enforcement effort."

The court of appeals then filed a new opinion, in which it retreated from its earlier statement. But the telltale chink in the armor had been there for all to see.

The attempt to discourage undercover investigations of corrupt judges in the original appeals court opinion in the *Archer* case hardly reflected the overriding concern for integrity one would have expected in the justice system. For a brief time, a panel of Federal judges seemed to be saying that a different set of rules applies when you are investigating dishonesty in the courts.

This question of *attitude* is the key to the elimination of corrupt practices. Honest judges must welcome the prosecution of corrupt judges. Honest lawyers must welcome the prosecution of corrupt lawyers. The same goes for businessmen, police officers, and all other groups. Fortunately, New York City had an extremely able police commissioner in the person of Patrick V. Murphy when the Knapp Commission disclosures came along. Murphy cooperated fully with the U. S. Attorney in undercover investigations of corruption in the courts and in his own department. He initiated many effective changes in police procedure and responsibility to help curb misconduct. Above all, he demonstrated to his men an *attitude* of strong opposition to corruption which told them he meant business.

There are others who actively resist efforts at eliminating corruption. In New York City, the Patrolmen's Benevolent Association supplies counsel to all police officers who are called as witnesses in corruption probes, and these lawyers follow a pattern of advising their "clients" never to assist such investigations. Spokesmen for the PBA counterattack whenever any effort is made to unearth police corruption.

Similar problems exist in other cities. In March, 1974, the Pennsylvania Crime Commission charged that police corruption in Philadelphia was "ongoing, widespread, systematic, and occurring at all levels of the Police Department." The commission, in a 1,404-page report, blamed a large part of the city's corruption problem on the attitude of Mayor Frank L. Rizzo, himself a former policeman. It was alleged that his administration had actively attempted to block the investigation and had failed to act on specific cases of corruption when they were presented. The commission called for the appointment of a special prosecutor to deal effectively with police corruption.*

Overwhelmingly, cases where corruption has been unearthed and successfully prosecuted have been those where an outside investigative body—often the Federal Government—has been

---

* The special prosecutor who was subsequently selected for the job was Walter M. Phillips, Jr., chief of the Narcotics Unit in the U. S. Attorney's office in the Southern District of New York.

involved. In New York City, it was the Knapp Commission and a special state prosecutor—plus the United States Attorney's office. In Baltimore, Newark, Chicago, Detroit, Pittsburgh, New Orleans, and many other cities, it has repeatedly been the U. S. Attorney's office that has provided the outside agency with the capability and objectivity to get the job done. The reason is evident. When the police department is corrupt, who can police it? When the criminal investigators are corrupt, who can investigate them? When the prosecutors are corrupt, who can prosecute them? As long as law enforcement power is kept in the hands of those who are themselves corrupt, the public interest is frustrated. The only hope lies in vesting jurisdiction in an outside body that has the capacity and will to investigate and prosecute as needed.

9

YEARNING TO BE FREE

In December, 1971, the tenants of a middle-income housing project in New York City formed the Bridge Apartments Tenants Association to oppose projected rent increases by the landlord and to seek improvement in maintenance, protection, and other tenant services. The middle-income housing project was constructed and financed under special housing legislation of New York State and supervised by the State Department of Housing and Community Renewal. A housewife from the project was elected chairman of the tenants' committee. Less than one week later, someone entered the chairman's apartment between three and four o'clock in the morning and removed several large appliances. Police investigating the incident noted that the perpetrators had locked the only access door to the apartment behind them, indicating that they had a master key.

On September 7, 1972, the tenants association chairman met with her attorneys, representatives of the building's management, and several employees to discuss protective services and maintenance schedules. Later that night, unknown persons entered the locked garage where the chairman's family parked their automobile and poured nearly five pounds of sugar into the gas tank. Fortunately, an alert gas-station attendant noticed loose sugar around the gas cap the following morning and repairs were made before the sugar had permanently damaged the engine.

Six weeks later, the tenant chairman met again with representatives of the management company and other members of the tenants association to discuss tenant grievances. Three days following, on Sunday, October 29, 1972, the chairman and her husband went to the garage to take out their car and discovered that the front windshield had been smashed. The next morning, the husband found the rear window of the car broken and all four tires slashed. No other tenant's vehicle had been touched.

On November 1, 1972, the distraught husband sent copies of a detailed letter describing these incidents to a number of public officials. One copy of the letter was received by our office. I referred it to the Assistant Attorney General in charge of the Civil Rights Division in Washington and recommended that the FBI investigate a possible violation of the Federal civil rights law. The Civil Rights Division did not respond for nearly a month, but finally wrote expressing doubt about Federal jurisdiction and concluding, therefore, that an FBI investigation would be "premature." The U. S. Attorney's office subsequently sent a detailed memorandum to Washington explaining why the Federal Government was entitled to proceed in the matter, but the Division would not budge.

Under existing civil rights statutes, only the Attorney General has the power to institute enforcement actions. By departmental directive, that authority has been delegated to the Civil Rights Division in the Department of Justice. The U. S. Attorney has the power to initiate investigations and prosecutions in every field of Federal law enforcement except civil rights, internal security, and election-law matters. As a result, a U. S. Attorney is powerless even to request an FBI investigation without prior approval of the Civil Rights Division. In fact, a U. S. Attorney is expressly *prohibited* under departmental regulations from issuing subpoenas or questioning witnesses before a grand jury in a civil rights matter without advance authorization.

There is no other significant area of Federal law enforcement in which local initiative by U. S. Attorneys is as hampered as in the field of civil rights. Even when the Civil Rights Division staff displays good faith, enforcement is slow and cumbersome. When any member of the division uses obstructionist tactics, for whatever reason, the entire process comes to a halt.

When civil rights legislation was first enacted and the country was subjected to a period of violence, it made sense to centralize control of civil rights enforcement. Most U. S. Attorneys' offices did not possess the manpower to commit to this extra effort, and in many Southern communities U. S. Attorneys did not have much enthusiasm for it, either.

But times have changed. Men like John Doar and Burke Marshall are no longer running the Civil Rights Division. With the passage of years it has become another bureaucracy, with a large staff and very little movement. In September, 1972, the Attorney General reported that there were 337 employees in the Civil Rights Division, 157 of whom were attorneys. During the preceding fiscal year the division had been involved in 206 new cases—less than one and one-half per attorney. During that fiscal year the Civil Rights Division had reviewed approximately sixteen thousand complaints of alleged criminal interference with the civil rights of citizens. These complaints resulted in twenty-five hundred investigations, which led to seventy-four grand jury presentations and indictments of ninety-two defendants. By the end of the fiscal year, nineteen persons had been convicted. Hardly a very impressive record for a staff of 157 lawyers.

Statistics aside, the actual performance by the Civil Rights Division has been alarmingly bad during the past few years. In the Southern District of New York, one of the busiest in the country, not one single case was referred from the Civil Rights Division in a three-year span. All civil rights enforcement activity was initiated by the U. S. Attorney's office itself, with no support and virtually no assistance from Washington. Worse than that, repeated requests for technical aid went unheeded for months, many of them forever. When investigations were completed and formal complaints prepared, the process of obtaining clearance from Washington was long and painful. Some enforcement actions were suspended with no affirmative action taken. When responses were forthcoming, they were characterized by faultfinding and excuses for failing to proceed.

The slowdown in the Civil Rights Division may well have reflected a deliberate policy of President Nixon. The United States Commission on Civil Rights filed a lengthy report on February 9, 1973. The commission criticized the Nixon Administration's lack of adequate enforcement of civil-rights laws: "This latest Commission study has reinforced the findings of the three preceding reports that the Government's civil rights program is not adequate or even close to it."

Whatever the reason, the Civil Rights Division is now an obstacle to vigorous civil rights enforcement. The time has come to reorganize and to vest general civil rights enforcement powers in the U. S. Attorneys as with other Federal statutes.

One can study the Civil Rights Division at work through its response to the 1970 beating of student anti-war demonstrators on the steps of Federal Hall in New York City. The building, a Federal structure, is on the site where George Washington took the first oath of office as President of the United States, and where Congress gave preliminary approval to the Bill of Rights. One of the rights guaranteed in that document is the right of assembly. On May 8, 1970, helmeted construction

179

workers broke up a students' anti-war demonstration, chasing youths through the financial district in a melee that left seventy persons injured. The workers then stormed City Hall, and forced officials to raise the American flag from half staff, where it had been placed in mourning for four students killed at Kent State University the previous Monday. Both the Mayor's office and the police department had received advance warning that several hundred construction workers would attack the peace demonstrators. The whole assult had obviously been well planned.

One construction worker told a *New York Times* reporter that not only were the workmen organized but in at least one case they had been offered a monetary bonus by their contractor-employers if they would take time off to "break some heads."

> According to the same construction worker, who said he wished to remain anonymous for fear of his life, he called the police at 8:30 A.M. yesterday and warned them that "construction workers are out for blood today, that construction jobs in lower Manhattan were going to be in on the bloodbath."
>
> A short time later, at about 9 A.M., Harriet Eisman, a special assistant to Representative Lowenstein, called a similar warning to City Hall. She said she had received a tip on Thursday night.
>
> "Last night I received a call from a friend of mine," Mrs. Eisman recalled. "He said that the workers were briefed by the shop stewards at the jobs to go and knock the heads of the kids who were protesting the Nixon-Kent thing."

On the day of the incident, the director of the New York Civil Liberties Union reported the attack to the U. S. Attorney's office. Other citizens filed complaints with our office, some in writing, some by phone, some in person. A list of witnesses was supplied. As the U. S. Attorney, I immediately called the Assistant Director of the FBI in New York and requested that an investigation be initiated to determine whether there had been a willful violation of federally protected civil rights.

Nothing happened.

Upon inquiry, the FBI said it had relayed the request to the Department of Justice for approval and had not yet received clearance to initiate an investigation. Four days later, I telephoned the Civil Rights Division to speed up approval of the investigation by the FBI. Still no action. Next came a series of meetings and communications urging the Civil Rights Division to move. Representatives of the division said that since a local investigation was being conducted by the police department it would be undesirable for the FBI to interfere. I continued to press the matter with letters, telephone calls, and meetings. I was particularly troubled that a delay would result in the disappearance of witnesses and evidence. Such investigations depend on people's recollections and the ability to locate witnesses. With each passing day the task grows more difficult. I expressed this concern repeatedly in letters to the Civil Rights Division.

Despite these pleas for action, the Civil Rights Division would not move. Finally, in January, 1971, I received a carbon copy of an official form headed "Notice to Close File." The document was signed by K. William O'Connor, the conservative chief of the Criminal Section in the Civil Rights Division. Incredibly, the main reason given for not proceeding with the investigation was that after such a long delay it would be difficult to locate witnesses.

> The very transitory nature of the construction industry in New York makes it extremely unlikely that the construction workers who were on the job sites and may have been involved in the march on May 8, 1970, would still be available in January or February, 1971. The resource commitment to this kind of investigation would be extensive, and I do not think it would be justified.

Exactly eight months had elapsed since the first request for investigation had been made.

PROTECTING THE RIGHTS OF THE POOR

To many people, Phillip Bialo might have seemed some sort of magician. Bialo was a professional process server. In a case in the Civil Court of the City of New York he filed an affidavit saying that he had attempted to serve a summons and complaint on Anna Ricon at her home address on February 26, February 28, March 4, and March 11, 1972. Finally, he swore, on March 13, 1972, he affixed a copy of the summons and complaint on Anna Ricon's front door, at 985 Simpson Street in the Bronx. What made the feat so miraculous was that the building at 985 Simpson Street had been demolished nine months before. His pattern was similar in many other cases. When he was indicted by the U. S. Attorney's office, Mr. Bialo pleaded guilty to seventeen counts of violating the Federal mail fraud statute, the Civil Rights Act and the Soldiers and Sailors Civil Relief Act. Bialo was sent to jail for one year

Phillip Bialo had been engaged in "sewer service." Professional process servers claim to deliver copies of summonses and complaints to individual defendants as required by state law, but instead they throw the papers "down the sewer." The defendant never knows he is being sued. When he fails to show up in court, the plaintiff enters a default judgment against him and then sends the sheriff or U. S. Marshal out to collect it. The most common mode of collection is to garnishee the defendant's wages if he is working at a regular job. Other collection procedures include seizing television sets, living-room furniture, or other household goods. The procedures are harsh. When these collection measures are combined with a deliberate failure to give a copy of the summons and complaint to the defendant, it is a plain denial of Constitutional due process.

Sewer service has been going on for a long time. In its monumental study of the causes of the racial strife in the mid-sixties, the Kerner Commission identified unfair credit and collection practices as one of the causes of frustration and unrest in urban ghettos. Nonetheless, the pattern of unfair collection practices has continued.

A study of consumer cases in the New York City Civil Court in November, 1973, revealed that 74 percent of the people sued in installment-credit cases have default judgments entered against them. Frequently, defendants against whom default judgments have been entered say that they never received a summons, but this could be because they did not recognize the significance of the flimsy piece of paper as a court document. Some process servers claim to deliver summonses to more than a hundred defendants in one day. One man claimed he visited 126 homes in a single day and found no one at home in any of them. Such claims are inherently unbelievable, but they do not provide a solid basis for taking affirmative criminal action.

The recent crackdown on dishonest process servers in New York grew out of the creation, in 1970, of a Consumer Protection Unit in the U. S. Attorney's office. Head of the unit was Assistant U. S. Attorney Patricia M. Hynes. In addition to the conviction of Bialo, Ms. Hynes also brought about the prosecution of George Wasserman, under a thirty-two-count indictment. Among the charges against Wasserman were his claims that he personally served Richard Rosenblatt at his home in the Bronx on October 7, 1972, when Mr. Rosenblatt was in Africa; that he had a conversation with Mrs. John K. Uhl as to whether her husband was in military service, when in fact Mrs. Uhl had been a deaf mute since birth; and that he had a conversation with Mrs. John McFadden on August 14, 1972, when both of the McFaddens were in England. Wasserman was convicted after a jury trial.

Assembling the evidence to support such prosecutions is a

mammoth job. In the case of Bialo and Wasserman it was accomplished through a detailed study of approximately twenty-five-thousand court files in the civil courts in Manhattan and Bronx counties to identify specific cases where positive proof of fraudulent affidavits of service could be established.

What is particularly unfair about such dishonest collection practices is that many debtor-defendants have valid legal defenses. Frequently they have received merchandise in damaged condition, or have been sold used merchandise misrepresented as new. Other valid reasons for nonpayment may exist, such as sickness or being laid off a job. Without proper service there is no opportunity to present such defenses. After a default judgment has been entered, it is virtually impossible to obtain legal assistance to undo the damage.

What these and other cases show is that dedication and imagination in a law enforcement office can achieve important goals in contemporary society. This consumer enforcement program was not the result of congressional enactments, White House policy, or Justice Department directive. It was conceived, staffed, and implemented by a local U. S. Attorney's office concerned about wrongs that needed something done about them.

FIGHTING JOB DISCRIMINATION

> Warring on poverty, inadequate housing, and employment is warring on crime. A civil rights law is a law against crime. Money for schools is money against crime. Medical, psychiatric, and family counselling services are services against crime. More broadly and more importantly, every effort to improve life in America's inner cities is an effort against crime.

This was a major conclusion of the President's Commission on Law Enforcement and Administration of Justice, headed by former Attorney General Nicholas deB. Katzenbach, in its final report, in 1967. In 1970, U. S. Judge A. Leon Higginbottom, commenting on causes of social unrest, noted that in poverty areas the unemployment rate among nonwhite teenagers was 34.2 percent—twice that of whites. In other neighborhoods, he said, the unemployment of nonwhites was 29 percent, compared to 13.8 percent for whites. "Wherever you go," the judge commented, "the unemployment rate is generally double for blacks as compared to whites."

The principal avenue of self-help for the urban poor is better jobs, which bring in more money and provide an opportunity for the poor family to move to a better neighborhood, send its children to better schools, and achieve economic security, which is the traditional cornerstone of the law-abiding American family. As long as artificial barriers stand in the way of workers' advancing themselves through their own abilities and effort, the syndrome that generates crime, and the bitterness and frustration that justify it, will be with us.

In 1970, the U. S. Attorney's office in New York undertook a program to end job discrimination in the construction industry. The idea grew from a settlement in a 1968 case fought under Title VII of the Civil Rights Act of 1964, prohibiting discrimination in employment. The action had been filed against the Wood, Wire and Metal Lathers International Union, Local 46, and the Joint Apprenticeship Committee of the Employing Metallic Furring and Lathing Association. The Federal action sought an injunction against the traditional construction industry pattern of discrimination as practiced by Local 46 and the JAC. On February 25, 1970, a settlement was filed under which the union agreed to admit twenty-five nonwhite apprentices immediately, to invalidate its existing discriminatory apprenticeship list, and to develop job opportunities. The consent decree provided a glimpse of what might be accomplished by a creative law enforcement program on a broader scale to break down existing job barriers in the construction industry. In terms of practical impact, opening up a single union with only sixteen hundred members did not go very far, but the potential for extending the approach throughout the industry was impressive. The Federal attorneys proceeded to compile a list of all crafts in the construction industry in the New York metropolitan area, and ranked them according to their 1970 hourly wage.

CRAFT	HOURLY WAGE PLUS BENEFITS
Structural Ironworkers	$10.76
Sheetmetal Workers	9.64
Bricklayers	9.55
Steamfitters	9.19
Ornamental Ironworkers	9.15
Carpenters	9.05
Roofers	9.03
Plumbers	8.94
Electrical Workers	8.91
Asbestos Workers	8.79
Operating Engineers	8.66
Metal Lathers	8.64
Plasterers	7.76
Laborers	7.34
Painters	6.88

The metal lathers were fourth from the bottom of the wage scale in the construction industry. But most job opportunities for nonwhite workers in the construction field were in the crafts with the lowest skills and lowest wages—plasterers, painters, and laborers.

The U. S. Attorney's office initiated an in-depth study of all construction craft unions in the metropolitan area. Lawyers visited every public and private agency concerned with discrimination; discussed complaints that had been received by the members of the staffs of these agencies; reviewed complaint files; assembled the names of witnesses who had been turned away from jobs in various fields. They also accumulated information on the membership of the unions in each of the major construction crafts, and reviewed official government reports filed by these unions to determine the percentage of nonwhite workers. What they found confirmed their suspicions. The principal opportunities for nonwhite blue-collar workers were in the low-paying jobs. The top wages went to workers in unions that were almost exclusively white.

The U. S. Attorney then set up a special team to tackle the task of ending job discrimination. Assistant U. S. Attorney Joel B. Harris was put in charge of a team of young lawyers backed by a group of research assistants, supplemented from time to time by law students and volunteers from the Brooklyn Heights Junior League.

The first civil rights cases filed against construction unions under the new program were announced on June 28, 1971. This group of cases represented four of the five top-paying craft unions in the construction industry. The prima facie proof of discrimination in these craft unions was dramatic. The following table shows the number of nonwhites in each union.

	TOTAL MEMBERSHIP	NONWHITE MEMBERSHIP
Local 638 (Steamfitters)	3850	31
Local 28 (Sheetmetal Workers)	3500	44
Local 580 (Ornamental Ironworkers)	1400	2
Local 40 (Structural Ironworkers)	878	50

The violations of Federal law included failure to admit nonwhite workers as journeymen members on the same basis as whites; failure to refer nonwhite workers for employment on the same basis as whites; failure to recruit nonwhites for membership on the same basis as whites; failure to permit contractors to hire the required number of nonwhite workers in compliance with Federal laws; and failure to take reasonable steps to notify nonwhite workers of employment opportunities.

187

Several months later two more building trades unions were the subject of additional proceedings. The unions strenuously resisted these efforts at removing racial barriers, but the Government won important victories one by one. Early in 1972, Judge Dudley B. Bonsal ordered Local 638 of the Steamfitters to take in qualified minority workers as full union members, and to achieve a minimum goal of 30 percent nonwhite membership by July 1, 1977. During the hearing, several thousand construction workers demonstrated in Foley Square, in front of the U. S. Courthouse, in an effort to block the judge's action. A few months later, Judge Murray I. Gurfein directed Local 40 of the Structural Ironworkers to admit all certified welders into the union immediately; to prepare and administer an impartial journeyman's examination for experienced blacks and Puerto Ricans; and to revise the union's hiring-hall procedures in order to insure a more equitable distribution of available jobs.

By January, 1974, Assistant U. S. Attorney Joel B. Harris reported that minority group membership in Local 638 of the Steamfitters had jumped from 31 to 880, a staggering rise in the light of past practices. Over eight hundred blacks and Spanish-surnamed workers had achieved job equality and human dignity in a few months in a single union, thanks to the determination and hard work of a handful of Assistant U. S. Attorneys.

Meanwhile, the original settlement with the metal-lathers' union had gone awry. The Government went back to court, and District Judge Marvin E. Frankel held the union in contempt.

It was the first time in the history of Federal civil rights enforcement that a union had been held in contempt of court for not meeting its obligations. In addition to ordering sweeping changes in the operation of the union's hiring hall, Judge Frankel awarded back pay to all minority workers who had been discriminated against. The U. S. Attorney's office prepared and submitted claims on behalf of ninety-five nonwhite workers, who obtained total recoveries in excess of one hundred thousand dollars. The judge also directed the union to issue at least 250 new work permits each year, through 1975, on a one-to-one ratio—issuing one permit to a nonwhite worker for every permit issued to a white worker. Through this procedure, the court undertook to undo some of the past damage. The order served as notice to the world that Federal law enforcement has the capacity to take whatever steps are necessary to insure social justice as well as justice under law.

10

PENTAGON PAPERS REVISITED

At 7:15 on the morning of Tuesday, June 15, 1971, the telephone rang in my motel room in Washington, D.C. Still only half-awake, I reached over and picked up the receiver. A male voice announced, "This is the White House switchboard. I have a call for you from Assistant Attorney General Mardian."

Robert C. Mardian, recently named head of the Internal Security Division in the Department of Justice, was brusque. "Where have you been?" he demanded. "We have been calling your room every half hour since midnight." I had just arrived in Washington the previous evening, for the Annual Conference of U. S. Attorneys. Apparently, the motel operator had been mistakenly ringing the telephone in the adjoining room, occupied by my teen-age children. The children had slept right through the noise.

Mardian explained that Attorney General Mitchell had sent off a telegram to *The New York Times* the previous evening requesting the newspaper to halt publication of its series on the secret Defense Department study on the war in Vietnam, which had first appeared in the *Times* two days before. The

Times had refused the request, he said, and therefore it was necessary to institute legal proceedings.

Mardian told me that the study had been unlawfully obtained by the *Times*. He added the papers contained a substantial number of extremely sensitive documents that directly affected national security. Mardian asked that the Southern District obtain a court order blocking further publication of the documents. He also wanted their return. He had already discussed the matter with the Chief Assistant in New York, Silvio J. Mollo, he said, and a crew of lawyers had been working through the night at the Department doing research and drafting legal papers.

After my conversation with Mardian, I conferred at length by telephone with Silvio Mollo and Michael D. Hess, Chief of the Civil Division. They discussed the procedures to be followed and the various steps that would have to be taken. A few hours later, the Government instituted *United States v. New York Times Company, et al.*, Civil Action 71-2662, in the Southern District of New York—one of the most hotly contested Constitutional litigations in modern times.

The action was not only to mark a milestone in First Amendment litigation, but it was also to unleash a chain of events in the name of "national security" which contributed to the collapse of the Presidency. The subsequent arrest and prosecution of Daniel Ellsberg, the creation of the "plumbers unit" in the White House to stop leaks, and the unmasking of the reckless misuse of executive power provided an alarming object lesson for all Americans.

The first legal step in the Pentagon Papers case was the filing of a complaint and motion papers seeking a temporary restraining order and preliminary injunction. The application for the interim order was argued before the United States District Court that very afternoon, Tuesday, June 15.

District Judge Murray I. Gurfein signed a temporary restraining order, enjoining further publication of the secret

documents until 1:00 P.M. on Saturday, June 19, and directed
the parties to appear for a full hearing on the Government's
application for a preliminary injunction on Friday, the 18th.
Meanwhile, the U. S. Attorney's staff was moving quickly to
gather all the facts it could. Henry Kissinger's office in the
White House called Michael Hess to impress on him the importance of the case. John Dean called with the same message.

On Friday morning, the hearing on the Government's application for a preliminary injunction got under way before Judge
Gurfein in a cavernous courtroom on Foley Square, in New
York City. The courtroom was bursting with observers, most
of them carrying press credentials. The tightly packed crowd
overflowed into the corridors. Unlike the usual, sedate court
proceeding, this one had the atmosphere of a sporting event,
with partisan murmurs of approval or boos, as *Times* lawyers
and the Government counsel, respectively, argued their positions.

The New York Times did not produce any witnesses at the
hearing, but instead submitted a large volume of affidavits,
primarily concerning the practice of leaking classified material
to the press and the abuse of "top secret" classifications on
Government papers. The Government called four witnesses,
who testified about the classification procedure currently in
use in the Defense establishment, and the presidential executive orders of the Eisenhower and Kennedy Administrations
under which classification had been carried out. They also described in a general fashion the contents of the forty-seven-
volume study on the Vietnam War, which had been classified
"top secret" because of the internal references to a number of
top secret documents.

During the afternoon, the court held an *in camera* hearing
in another courtroom from which everyone was excluded except
representatives of the Government and *The New York Times*.
Evidence was submitted on some of the specific sensitive prob-

lems presented by the threatened disclosure of documents contained in the Defense Department study.

At the outset of the hearing on Friday, June 18, the *Times'* counsel, Professor Alexander Bickel, of Yale Law School, made a motion to dismiss the entire proceeding on the ground that it was moot and dramatically announced that the *Washington Post* had just begun publication of the same classified documents. With a flourish, Professor Bickel handed copies of the *Washington Post* and the *New York Post* to Judge Gurfein. Assistant Attorney General Mardian immediately told the Government lawyers to advise Judge Gurfein that the Government would take steps to initiate a companion action against the *Washington Post* in the District of Columbia. So began the see-saw legal proceedings in New York City and Washington, D.C., which arrived on the doorstep of the Supreme Court almost simultaneously a few days later.

On Saturday afternoon, June 19, Judge Gurfein called counsel into his book-lined chambers and handed out copies of a sixteen-page opinion denying the Government's request for a preliminary injunction. Judge Gurfein told the lawyers that Judge Irving R. Kaufman, of the U. S. Court of Appeals, was in his chambers in the building, and was available for "any application." That same day, Judge Kaufman issued a brief order extending the district court's temporary restraining order until Monday at noon, to permit a full three-judge panel of the court of appeals to consider the application for a stay pending appeal. On Monday morning, Chief Judge Henry J. Friendly advised the parties that the matter would be set down for argument before all eight judges of the court of appeals, sitting *en banc,* the following afternoon.

Meanwhile, the Government had instituted proceedings in the District of Columbia to enjoin further publication of classified documents in the *Washington Post.* That application had been denied in the district court and was scheduled for argument in the U. S. Court of Appeals for the District of Columbia simultaneously with the argument in New York. As its main ground of appeal, the Government argued that Judge Gurfein had not sufficiently examined the seven-thousand-page classified study to warrant his conclusion that no damage to the national security would result from its publication.

On Wednesday afternoon, June 23, the Court of Appeals, in a 5-to-3 decision, reversed Judge Gurfein's ruling and ordered the case sent back for more testimony and findings. The appellate court directed the Government to submit no later than June 25 a detailed list of specific portions of the study it claimed would damage the national security. The court also authorized *The New York Times* to proceed with the publication of any documents not so specified by the Government after that date. Judge Gurfein was directed to conduct further *in camera* proceedings to determine whether dislosure of any of the items specified by the Government "pose such grave and immediate danger to the security of the United States as to warrant their publication being enjoined."

On the following day, *The New York Times* filed a petition for certiorari in the Supreme Court of the United States. On Friday, the petition was granted, and the case was set down for oral argument the very next day. Simultaneously, certiorari was granted in the companion case involving the *Washington Post,* with argument of the two cases to be heard together.

A historic special Saturday session of the Supreme Court of the United States was held in Washington, D.C., on June 26, 1971. Solicitor General Erwin N. Griswold urged that an injunction should issue against the publication of ten specific groups of documents which vitally affected current military and diplomatic operations, in order to permit the carrying out of the Executive's responsibilities under Article II of the Constitution. Counsel for the *Times* and the *Post* argued that the First Amendment to the Constitution forbade any enjoining of such publication.

On Wednesday, four days later, the Supreme Court broke tradition again—the nine Justices filed ten opinions, one written on behalf of the Court and the others each written by an individual member. Six Justices voted against enjoining publication of the documents, for varying reasons; three Justices dissented.

United States v. New York Times Company created a conflict of interest problem for the *Times* itself. Here was the *Times,* party to an intensely controlled litigation, reporting and editorializing on that litigation to the public at large. Other newspapers and newscasters, all emotionally identifying with the *Times'* cause, were likewise reporting on a legal battle in which they were simultaneously engaging as advocacy journalists. The result was predictable—despite varying degrees of effort at maintaining objectivity, an overriding bias crept into both reporting and editorial columns. The public was misled about the real issues in the case. The word "censorship" was repeated over and over again. Throughout the press reports on the proceedings, the impression was created that the Government's position was simply a bald attempt to conceal from the American public the errors of earlier Administrations in the conduct of the Vietnam War.

The New York Times itself set the tone in the first of its several editorials commenting on the case:

> The documents in question belong to history. They refer to the development of American interest and participation in Indochina from the post-World War II period up to mid-1968, which is now almost three years ago. Their publication could not conceivably damage American security interests, much less the lives of Americans or Indochinese.

This theme, that the litigation only involved questions of history, was picked up and repeated everywhere. It was, in fact, a complete distortion of the issues presented in the case, as a reading of the court opinions plainly discloses. There was no problem about printing history. The problem arose with threatened publication of documents having a *current* impact on military operations and foreign relations.

The basis of the Government's request for an injunction was simply that the publication of *some* of the classified documents would damage the national security. The Government's real concern was that portions of the secret Defense Department study directly affected military and intelligence operations and secret diplomatic efforts to achieve peace. Several members of the Supreme Court recognized that the Government's position was right, including Justice White, who voted with the majority and with whom Justice Stewart joined in his concurring opinion.

> I do not say that in no circumstances would the First Amendment permit an injunction against publishing information about Government plans or operations. Nor, after examining the materials the Government characterizes as the most sensitive and destructive, can I deny that revelation of these documents will do substantial damage to public interests. Indeed, I am confident that their disclosure will have that result.

The Government's objective in seeking an injunction against publication of classified documents was not to prevent the disclosure of historic documents but to protect *current* operations in withdrawing American troops from Vietnam; *current* efforts to achieve and maintain peace in Southeast Asia; *current* negotiations to obtain the release of American prisoners of war; *current* efforts at avoiding further conflict in the Middle East and in Europe; and *current* and future efforts to achieve peace through the Strategic Arms Limitation Talks.

Another misconception generated by the news media's coverage of the *Times* case was that the case was without precedent. On the very day of the hearing in the district court, I received an unsolicited letter from Julian P. Boyd, editor of *The Papers of Thomas Jefferson,* published by the Princeton University Press, who supplied the following statement made by Jefferson on June 17, 1807, in a letter to U. S. Attorney George W. Hay of the District of Virginia:

> All nations have found it necessary that, for the advantageous conduct of their affairs, some of these proceedings, at least, should remain known to their Executive functionary only. He of course, from the nature of the case, must be the sole judge of which of them the public interests will permit publication.

The Jefferson letter to Hay was sent during the trial of Aaron Burr for treason, presided over by Chief Justice John Marshall. Burr's counsel had moved for the issuance of a subpoena to compel Jefferson to turn over a letter that the President had written to an Army general. The position espoused by Jefferson was the same one that Government counsel argued in the *Times* case—that documents affecting the national security should not be published if the Executive believes that publication would damage the country's welfare.

A similar view had been expressed by George Washington when he declined a request from Congress to provide it with the papers leading up to the signing of the Jay Treaty.

> The nature of foreign negotiations requires caution, and their success must often depend on secrecy; and even when brought to a conclusion a full disclosure of all the measures, demands, or eventual concessions which may have been proposed or contemplated would be extremely impolitic; for this might have a pernicious influence on future negotiations, or produce immediate inconveniences, perhaps danger and mischief, in relation to other powers.

Actually, the Government had a pretty good judicial batting average in the *Times* case. Counting all of the judges in the district, circuit, and Supreme courts, a total of eight judges supported the Government's position while ten ruled the other way. (If you add in the *Washington Post* case, the score would be ten to eighteen—still far from a shutout.)

What is probably much more significant is the practical result of the litigation. During the course of the *in camera* proceedings before the District Court and Court of Appeals the Government identified for the court, and also for *The New York Times* and its counsel, those portions of the Defense Department study which would be most damaging currently to the nation's welfare. William B. Macomber, the State Department official who testified during the district court hearing, has since publicly noted that the material published by the newspapers following the Supreme Court decision did *not* include the particular designated portions that would have damaged national security. In fact, in the *Washington Post* case, the publisher voluntarily *agreed* in the U. S. district court *not* to publish the documents that posed serious security risks. In short, the Government attorneys actually *accomplished the results* they were after—halting the publication of the particular documents that presented a current threat to the nation's welfare. The Government had lost the battle but won the war.

The Government *won?* Hard to believe, but true. Nonetheless the news media continue to perpetuate the myth that the litigation was essentially a pointless effort at repression of history.

NATIONAL SECURITY PARANOIA

Undoubtedly the most sobering lesson of all, growing out of the Pentagon Papers case and many events that have happened since, is that the concept of "national security" can be converted into a governmental paranoia that is unhealthy and even dangerous. National security is a genuine menace when it serves as the rationalization for illegal wiretaps of newsmen and attempts to steal privileged medical records.

There can be no doubt that the fundamental concept that motivated *The New York Times* reporters was correct—there is too much over-classification of documents in Government and too much inertia in releasing those which should be in the public domain. The only thing wrong was the way the *Times* went about declassifying the documents. The concept was right. The procedure was wrong.

The particular officials who have been involved in national security also give real grounds for concern. Government must be run by men of reason and good will. Some of the practices of Federal security personnel are wholly irrational and dangerous if employed in the wrong context. The security officers themselves undoubtedly never saw the humor of it. However, to the government lawyers working on the *Times* case, the fixation about security clearances and guarding of documents was at times comic opera. Room 401 in the U. S. Courthouse on Foley Square became an armed camp, as Defense Department guards were stationed at the entrance to challenge all who approached.

During the preparation of the witnesses to testify at the first hearing before District Judge Gurfein in New York—all of them senior representatives of the Defense and State Departments—the prospective witnesses were asked to identify the specific documents contained in the study which would jeopardize national security. The reply from the Defense Department counsel, J. Fred Buzhardt, was classic. "They cannot tell you," he said. "The information is classified."

Impossible as it may be to believe, the Defense and State Department representatives simply would not explain to the government lawyers which of the documents in the forty-seven volumes of the Pentagon Papers presented specific risks to national security, although they were absolutely positive that such documents existed. Throughout the evening and early morning of the hearing, Buzhardt (who was later to be detailed to the White House as counsel to President Nixon during the controversy over the Oval Office tapes in the Watergate investigation) was adamant. Not only would he *not* let the witnesses tell government counsel which documents were the most sensitive, he said he would *not even* let them tell the judge, unless everyone else was cleared out of the courtroom. The fact that this would have meant that the *Times* would be denied its Constitutional right of confrontation and cross-examination of witnesses did not faze him one bit. He simply would not budge from his position.

Eventually, after wasting precious hours in argument with Buzhardt, the witnesses did agree to describe the nature of the sensitive documents, in broad categories. But never once would they agree to identify specific documents. Hence, the U. S. Attorney and his staff could present the court with only this limited information about the security risks in the Pentagon Papers, and hope that it would be enough to enable the judge to identify the specific documents that would damage the nation's current military and diplomatic operations.

After Judge Gurfein's decision denying the Government a preliminary injunction, the Defense Department representatives were dumbstruck. They had lived in the never-never land where their word was law. The idea that someone else might *not* accept their word about a national security problem was unthinkable. Now the White House got into the act. John Dean, who had been assigned to follow the case, called the U. S. Attorney's office on Saturday afternoon after the decision, to see if he could do anything to help. I got on the phone and explained to him the roadblocks that had been thrown up by Buzhardt, which had made it impossible to present a detailed case. He promised to do something about it. When what had happened finally dawned on the Defense Department brass, they were suddenly ready to help the lawyers with specifics. Admiral Blouin provided the U. S. Attorney's office with a detailed affidavit specifying the documents that presented current security risks. At last the government lawyers had something they could argue from effectively. The problem was that it came too late. Whether the outcome of the whole case might have been different if the Pentagon witnesses had provided the specific identification of sensitive documents at the outset is anyone's guess. But the experience does demonstrate the totally unreal world in which the national security specialists function.

When Solicitor General Erwin Griswold was preparing the Government's *in camera* brief for submission to the Supreme Court on the night before the argument, the security men told him that the Solicitor General's secretary had not received a security clearance and therefore could not type the brief. Dean Griswold's patience snapped. He told the security officers to inform their supervisor that the Solicitor General of the United States chose not to follow his instructions. A guard spent the night camped outside the Solicitor General's door.

As chief of the Internal Security Division of the Department of Justice, Robert Mardian was widely regarded both inside and outside the Department as a dangerous man. His constant emphasis on using the criminal justice system to repress activities by "subversives" was a source of genuine concern. Under Mardian's direction, Guy Goodwin, the chief of the Special Litigation section of the Internal Security Division, traveled around the country appearing in one Federal district after another to convene special grand juries and conduct freewheeling probes into left-wing organizations with little apparent regard for the rights of witnesses. During the course of less than two years, Guy Goodwin personally conducted grand jury investigations in Seattle, Washington; Harrisburg, Pennsylvania; Camden, New Jersey; Tyler, Texas; Kansas City, Missouri; Tallahassee, Florida; Ogden, Utah; Tucson, Arizona; San Francisco, California; Chicago, Illinois; Detroit, Michigan, and Portland, Oregon. He produced indictments against 105 defendants in this whirlwind tour and left behind him a trail of outraged government and private lawyers.

Mardian's role in the Pentagon Papers case was chilling. From the very outset, his heavy-handedness forced a confrontation between the Government and the press which was probably totally unnecessary. Instead of trying to meet quietly and privately with one of the executives at the *Times* to alert the publishers to the small group of sensitive documents which was buried in the forty-seven-volume study, he persuaded the Attorney General to send off a bluntly worded telegram *demanding* that publication of the entire study be halted. It was like sending a challenge to a duel—the adversary had no choice but to respond in kind.

Undoubtedly, there were those in the Nixon palace guard who were secretly delighted at the prospect of going after *The New York Times* to get even for the unfavorable editorials and unbalanced news stories that had appeared steadily ever since the Republicans had come into office, but that was no way to deal with a genuine issue of national security. There were many career people in Washington who sincerely believed that full disclosure of the contents of the Pentagon Papers would damage national defense. Someone should have zeroed in on the most sensitive documents and simply gone to the *Times* and explained why it would hurt the country's interests to print those particular papers. Although the *Times* itself had been as much at fault as Mardian in not asking Defense or State Department experts whether any such documents existed, there are nevertheless numerous top executives at the *Times* who are responsible citizens and who would certainly have listened to reason if properly approached.

Mardian had a different view. His position was simply that the executive branch had classified these documents as "top secret" and that ended the matter. To disclose their contents was illegal, and anyone who did so was violating the law. Period. When the injunction proceeding came on for hearing before Judge Gurfein, Mardian came to New York to be in the courtroom. When I stood up to argue for the Government that the court could decide for itself whether the classification had been properly placed, Mardian was incensed. He noisily whispered in my ear that the Executive had classified the documents, and that was controlling. The court had *no choice* but to issue an injunction. He was angry that the Southern District office was once again taking its own independent stance.

The press, of course, reported the proceeding as if the Mardian approach *was* the Government's position. But the contrary was true. Against Mardian's wishes, we told Judge Gurfein that most of the study *could* be published despite its classification. Our only concern was about the particular documents that the career professionals said would seriously harm our national interests.

When the *Washington Post* took up publication of the study after the *Times* had been stayed by the district court's order, Mardian saw his chance to get the case under his control. Instead of joining the proceedings against the two newspapers in the same court (which was possible, since the *New York Post* was involved), Mardian started a separate injunction action in Washington using his own staff, where he could be free to present his hard-line position. The result was predictable. While we *won The New York Times* case in the court of appeals in New York, Mardian's staff *lost* the *Washington Post* case in the court of appeals in the District of Columbia. It was only a matter of time now before the whole proceeding would be over.

Nothing daunted, Mardian proceeded to lay plans to prosecute those who were responsible for the publication of the Pentagon Papers. He proposed to impanel three grand juries to hear testimony in the matter—one in Boston, one in Los Angeles, and one in New York. He telephoned Michael Hess in New York and offered him the position of Executive Assistant in the Internal Security Division to coordinate the entire investigation. Hess turned him down flat.

A few days later, Deputy Attorney General Richard Kleindienst came to New York to pay an official visit to our office.

I invited several of the top members of the staff to join me in taking him to lunch at Stark's Restaurant, on Broadway, not far from the courthouse. During the luncheon discussion, Kleindienst turned the conversation to the Pentagon Papers. "We're thinking of starting a grand jury investigation in New York to find out who at *The New York Times* was responsible for receiving the stolen documents from Ellsberg, so we can prosecute them," he said.

I turned to him and said simply, "Not in this District."

That was the end of the *Times* case as far as the U. S. Attorney was concerned. But the White House and the Department of Justice thought otherwise. As a result of the Pentagon Papers dispute, the White House set up the "plumbers unit." The Internal Security Division conducted grand jury investigations in Boston and Los Angeles which culminated in the indictment of Ellsberg.

The Ellsberg case came to trial in 1973, and while the jury was deliberating, the trial judge threw the case out. His principal reason was the filing of a Justice Department memorandum admitting that E. Howard Hunt, Jr., and G. Gordon Liddy, members of the White House "plumbers unit," during the very same period when Mardian was laying plans for his three-pronged grand jury probe, had illegally broken into the office of Ellsberg's psychiatrist and attempted to steal his file in hopes of discovering derogatory information. The Government's unlawful action, the judge said, had tainted the entire prosecution.

PARANOIA AT THE *TIMES*

Excessive secrecy, misuse of power, and invasion of personal rights in the name of national security can never be justified. It is healthy for the press to oppose this tendency in government. Abuses in government, however, do not justify abuses in the press. Excesses by editors and journalists also threaten the public interest.

Insight into dubious motives and actions of *Times* editors and reporters in the Pentagon Papers case is supplied in a candid book, *The Papers & the Papers*, by *Washington Post* reporter Sanford J. Ungar. Published in 1972, the book is based on interviews with many of the principals in the Pentagon Papers case. What the book reveals about behind-the-scenes operations at the *Times* is just as alarming as anything we know about the behind-the-scenes operations of the Internal Security Division and the national security zealots in the White House.

The obvious question in the mind of any responsible person deciding whether or not to publish classified government documents should be whether publication would damage foreign relations, secret negotiations, or military or intelligence operations. The *Times* never tried to find out. According to Ungar, the reason the editors failed to consult outside experts about possible national security dangers in publishing the Pentagon Papers was that the newspaper did not want to be scooped by anyone else. Daniel Ellsberg had delivered the stolen documents to *Times* reporter Neil Sheehan and had told him that Senator Fulbright also had a set of the papers, as did the Institute for Policy Studies, which was working on a book based on the information contained in the documents. This knowledge created strong pressure on Sheehan's boss, Max Frankel, then head of the *Times* Washington Bureau. Mr. Ungar wrote:

> Frankel feared that the *Times* would be scooped by a U. S. Senator or that the radical scholars at the institute would leak parts of the Papers to politicians they favored. He also found it inconceivable that the Papers would not soon fall into the hands of another newspaper, most likely either the *Washington Post* or the *Los Angeles Times*.

Once the Pentagon Papers project got under way, a secret headquarters was set up in the Hilton Hotel in New York City, with a special staff of *Times* reporters, editors, and production personnel going through the documents and preparing articles for eventual publication. The primary concern was to avoid being scooped. According to Mr. Ungar, "The reporters were warned not to phone any of the authors of the Papers or participants in the decision-making process on Vietnam to check details, lest the secret of the *Times* scoop got out."

The staff in the secret *Times* hideaway was under increasing pressure to produce copy for the Pentagon Papers series.

> They were under constant pressure from [Foreign Editor James L.] Greenfield and [Managing Editor A. M.] Rosenthal to produce copy, but despite twelve-to-fifteen-hour workdays the process moved even more slowly than expected. "We were just tormented by the notion that somebody else would dribble this stuff," Frankel says.

This compulsive drive to beat out other newspapers and be the first ones with the story gives quite a different complexion to the high-sounding proclamations about the "public's right to know" asserted in *Times* editorials.

What turned out to be so particularly ironic about the *Times*'s handling of the Pentagon Papers was its lofty criticism of excessive secretiveness on the part of government agencies, as contrasted to its own secretiveness in working on the Pentagon Papers project. The whole operation received the designation "Project X." The New York Hilton was picked as headquarters for Project X so that the reporters and editors would be anonymous among the large numbers of tourists and conventioneers. Reporters were brought surreptitiously into the New York area and then sent off to the hotel with instructions not to appear at the *Times* office, on 43rd Street, but to work only in the Hilton.

When the publishing deadline finally drew near, a group of rooms on the ninth floor of the *Times*' own building, far from the News Department, was set aside for Project X. The room was stripped of its furnishings, rugs, and curtains. The walls were lined with masonite. Typesetting machines and proof presses were moved in secretly. A *Times* security man was posted at the door with instructions to admit only those on a secret list. When the Sunday, June 13, 1971, issue of the *Times* was being prepared in the news room, a huge four-column blank was left in the middle of the front page. Six inside pages were also left blank. The type was finally wheeled into the main composing room and the paper went to press. Government agencies might learn a lesson or two from the *Times* when it comes to maintaining tight security.

Despite their protestations of "public duty," the *Times* people were very nervous about the public's reaction to what they were doing, and were determined to get the best possible image. Their image-making included persuading friends at another major newspaper to send a cable to the *Times* publisher, Arthur Sulzberger, who was then in London, congratulating him on the journalistic coup in publishing the Pentagon Papers. Then, without blinking an eye, the *Times* editors turned around and sanctimoniously charged government officials with deception.

When Judge Gurfein issued the original temporary restraining order halting *Times* publication of the Pentagon Papers, the *Washington Post* received a call from Daniel Ellsberg, which was routed to Assistant Managing Editor Ben Bagdikian. Bagdikian then made a flying visit to Boston, and after a series of furtive meetings, picked up a cardboard carton filled with Xerox copies of Pentagon Papers.

One would have supposed that when the *Washington Post* started publishing the Papers after the Federal court in New York had enjoined *The New York Times*, the *Times* people would have shouted "Hurrah!" in view of their stated concern about the "public's right to know" the contents of the Papers. But that was not the reaction at all. Managing Editor A. M. Rosenthal was quoted by Mr. Ungar as saying "I was jumping up and down in here like a madman." Neil Sheehan and the other reporters who had worked on the Pentagon Papers were angry that the *Post* was taking the glory away from them.

The *Times* people were so obsessed with being scooped, and hence so security-conscious, that they deliberately did not consult independent experts about possible damage to the nation's international operations from the publication of "top secret" documents. Was it so unreasonable for the Government to go to court and ask that publication be postponed until such expert opinions could be obtained and considered?

In the aftermath of the Pentagon Papers case, many newspaper people have expressed bitterness about the entire proceeding. They resent the fact that the *Times* and the *Post* were taken to court. They express deep concern that there was even a temporary "prior restraint" on their publishing installments in the Pentagon Papers series. This attitude deserves close scrutiny. In a popular democracy like ours, whatever one's personal views may be about the Administration in power, the filing of an application in the Federal courts, with full appellate rights for both sides to the Court of Appeals and to the Supreme Court of the United States, is *precisely* the right way to handle such a controversy. The notion that newspaper editors and publishers in a private, profit-making enterprise are "untouchables" whose actions may not be challenged in courts of law is contrary to the concept of a free democratic society. The control of newspapers and broadcast media provides enormous power—a power that is multiplied many times when the processes of attrition have reduced the number of journalistic voices. As a result, papers like *The New York Times* and the *Washington Post* dominate the flow of information for literally millions of citizens.

Power must be responsibly exercised, whether in government or in newspapers. When it is not, those who wield the power should be called to account. Any right-thinking person would reject the notion of government control over the news media.

Primary accountability for journalists should be to their own peers. But when they go beyond simple questions of responsible journalism and invade the provinces of others—such as the power of their government's duly selected officials to conduct diplomatic and military operations that require secrecy—then there must be some forum for challenging that conduct and bringing it into line with other constitutional responsibilities.

It was particularly ironic in the Pentagon Papers case that after having waited *three months* before going into print, *The New York Times* should be so outraged at the notion that publication be delayed for another few days while the courts gave mature consideration to the difficult questions that had been presented.

Now that the dust has settled and tempers have cooled, it might be appropriate for all concerned to look again at the very sensible language contained in the dissenting opinion of Chief Justice Warren Burger. That opinion pointed out how unreasonable it was for the *Times* to take so long to prepare to publish the Pentagon Papers and then suddenly demand that everybody else respond at breakneck speed. The Chief Justice also pointed out that the editors had acted irrationally in failing to get expert guidance as to those documents that might pose threats to national security. Had they done so, they could have avoided the confrontation entirely.

> It is not disputed that the *Times* has had unauthorized possession of the documents for three to four months, during which it has had its expert analysts studying them, presumably digesting them and preparing the material for publication. During all of this time, the *Times*, presumably in its capacity as trustee of the public's "right to know," has held up publication for purposes it considered proper and thus public knowledge was delayed. No doubt this was for a good reason; the analysis of 7,000 pages of complex material drawn from a vastly greater volume of material would inevitably take time and the writing of good news stories takes time.

But why should the United States Government, from whom this information was illegally acquired by someone, along with all the counsel, trial judges, and appellate judges be placed under needless pressure? After these months of deferral, the alleged right to know has somehow and suddenly become a right that must be vindicated instanter.

Would it have been unreasonable, since the newspaper could anticipate the Government's objections to release of secret material, to give the Government an opportunity to review the entire collection and determine whether agreement could be reached on publication? Stolen or not, if security was not in fact jeopardized, much of the material could no doubt have been declassified, since it spans a period ending in 1968.

With such an approach—one that great newspapers have in the past practised and stated editorially to be the duty of honorable press—the newspapers and Government might well have narrowed the area of disagreement as to what was and was not publishable, leaving the remainder to be resolved in orderly litigation if necessary. To me it is hardly believable that a newspaper long regarded as a great institution in American life would fail to perform one of the basic and simple duties of every citizen with respect to the discovery or possession of stolen property or secret Government documents. That duty, I had thought—perhaps naively—was to report forthwith, to responsible public officers. This duty rests on taxi drivers, justices and *The New York Times*. The course followed by the *Times,* whether so calculated or not, removed any possibility of orderly litigation of the issues.

11

POISONED PENS

Ordinary public officials should never expect to be loved by the press. *Toleration* is about the best they can hope for. The news media construe their responsibility as being "watchdog for the people." They should expose pomposity or malfeasance wherever it exists. Unfortunately, zeal often replaces sound judgment in this process, and the giddiness of power often leads small men to attack public officeholders for the sheer pleasure of cutting them down to size.

When the leadership of the U. S. Attorney's office in New York changed in early 1970, the event generated a considerable uproar in the press. Robert Morgenthau, the capable incumbent appointed by the prior, Democratic Administration, refused to resign following the election of the Republican national Administration. Finally, he was asked to leave. He did so under protest, attracting widespread press coverage of the controversy. News stories and editorials made dark predictions of imminent destruction of the U. S. Attorney's office in the hands of Morgenthau's Republican successor. Partisanship would become the order of the day. The office would soon be overrun with political hacks. Sinister hints of likely suppression of prosecutions, political favoritism, and just plain incompetence were freely offered by journalists. Even Ralph Nader came to New York expressly to hold a press conference to declare that banking interests were going to take control of the Federal prosecutor's office.

Meanwhile, as the incoming U. S. Attorney, I had quietly been working to counteract these unfair allegations by selecting an executive staff of unquestioned ability. I had already agreed during private conversations with my predecessor to keep on Morgenthau's Chief Assistant United States Attorney. There remained two other major posts to fill: the chiefs of the Criminal and Civil divisions. For the former post I selected a talented young lawyer who had previously been chosen by Morgenthau as chief of the Special Prosecutions Unit, responsible for investigating and prosecuting organized crime. For chief of the Civil Division, I chose another Morgenthau Assistant, who had previously served as a law clerk to a United States district judge. By chance, the Civil Division chief was an enrolled Republican.

Craig R. Whitney was *The New York Times* reporter assigned to the pressroom in the Federal courthouse during the time of the predictions that partisanship would soon run the U. S. Attorney's office. When the appointment of the three top staff executives was announced—refuting any suggestion of partisanship—Mr. Whitney nonetheless found a way to write the story which revealed extraordinary bias. Instead of reflecting the truly nonpolitical spirit of these appointments, Whitney zeroed in on the *only* Republican in the group, who, he wrote, "is described as having excellent Republican connections."

Whitney's story was calculated to prove the earlier dire predictions of political patronage in the staffing of the office. It was a cheap shot. Not only was the singling out of the lone Republican a perversion of truth; it was also a grave injustice to the young lawyer, who had just realized a long-time ambition to hold the top job in the Civil Division. He had been selected entirely on merit, but to the outside world, including his family and friends, *The New York Times* implied that he had been selected because of his "Republican connections."

Whitney continued to write stories about the U. S. Attorney's office for the *Times* over the course of many months. Although many of his stories had the same cast, apparently no editor ever called him on his biased reporting. Instead, he was promoted, to foreign correspondent. Three years later, a letter arrived at the U. S. Attorney's office with the return address of *The New York Times* bureau in Bonn, Germany. The letter, addressed to me, said:

> I must say you could not have done a better job of proving to me that you were not at the end of John Mitchell's string than by your indictment of him last week.
>
> I'm only sorry I didn't stay to redress my original misapprehensions. And sorrier that you won't be there "Four more years."
>
> Please accept my very best wishes and—I mean this—highest regard.
>
> Best,
>
> CRAIG R. WHITNEY

What a startling confession from a professional journalist! How can that letter possibly make up for the many months of biased reporting? How can it make up to the young lawyer who was appointed chief of the Civil Division for the grossly unfair newspaper story about what should have been a day of glory but for him turned out so bitter?

In 1972, an article by a free-lance writer in *The New York Times Magazine* described the problems of entry into construction unions by blacks and Puerto Ricans. The article referred to the enforcement effort that had been initiated in the U. S. Attorney's office in New York to undo these injustices. As originally submitted by the author, the article fairly credited the hard work by the staff of the U. S. Attorney's office in achieving a breakthrough in efforts to eliminate job discrimination. By now, the Pentagon Papers case had taken place, and *Times* editors carefully deleted any favorable mention of the U. S. Attorney's office. The author was so upset by the deletions that he wrote to the Assistant U. S. Attorney in charge of the civil rights enforcement program in the U. S. Attorney's office, sending along a copy of the original proof.

> I'm sending you the enclosed proof so that you and Robin can see what the Times—without informing me —cut from the construction article.
>
> Originally there was a good quote from you which they deleted in manuscript and wouldn't restore. I tell you this detail because I appreciated your cooperation and admire your efforts, and I don't want you to think I was insensitive to their importance.
>
> The specifics on case preparation are vital to any understanding of the difficulties in routing out union discrimination. Times' editors slicing with a machete have carved out material that should have been available to readers. I'm sorry. It was none of my doing.

"INVESTIGATIVE" REPORTING

"I love coming to work. Being the bad-ass. It's exhilarating. It's power." The words are those of David Burnham of *The New York Times,* one of the current crop of "investigative reporters." Investigative reporters like Burnham are the elite of journalism. They have been elevated to special prominence by the Pulitzer Prize-winning efforts of Carl Bernstein and Bob Woodward, the two young reporters on the *Washington Post* who unearthed the Watergate cover-up.

The problem is that there is a great confusion as to what really constitutes investigative reporting. Many such journalists make a specialty of simply publishing leaks about matters that are *not* being covered up. They make their living off tips from law enforcement officers about investigations that are currently under way.

For several years law enforcement officials in New York City have been concerned about indications of corruption in the criminal justice system. Intelligence from a number of sources has suggested the possibility of corruption in fixing cases not just on the police-officer level but ranging through bail bondsmen, private investigators, lawyers, assistant district attorneys, and even judges and their clerks. Intelligence information, however, is not a sufficient basis for criminal prosecutions, and assembling evidence of corruption on the part of those who control the enforcement machinery itself is virtually impossible without an inside contact. The only conceivable means for obtaining proof is through the participants themselves, who obviously have no interest in admitting their wrongdoing. Corrupt deals are made in secret, with every precaution taken to avoid detection. Moreover, the testimony of *one* participant to a bribe is rarely sufficient to provide a basis for a prosecution. No jury would take the word of a narcotics dealer against an upright police officer. No jury would accept the word of a single witness against a lawyer, or an assistant district attorney, or a judge. Such testimony must always be corroborated. Because of the circumstances under which most bribes are paid and fixes are arranged, it is almost impossible to overhear conversations or photograph participants. There are no fingerprints or incriminating documents. The one investigative procedure that has proved successful is to obtain a secret recording of the conversation through the cooperation of one of the participants, thereby supplying positive, objective proof of what actually happened. This means that one of the participants in a corrupt arrangement must wear a miniature tape recorder. Such recordings cannot be made after the fact. The only hope of getting solid corroborating evidence is by infiltrating a corrupt arrangement and persuading one participant to cooperate with law enforcement officers in obtaining the necessary proof.

Nicholas Scoppetta, an attorney on the staff of the Knapp Commission, was able to develop the confidence of a young city detective, Robert Leuci, who had been immersed in corruption practically from the first day he joined the police department. As a result, an opportunity of unparalleled proportions presented itself. Here was a man who could work under cover in cooperation with a government agency to bring an end to unbridled corruption of local law enforcement. More significant, Detective Leuci's principal areas of corrupt contacts were in the fields of narcotics and organized crime. New York City was the heroin capital of the United States, and the failure to prosecute effectively the black-market distribution network was one of the reasons why the problem of heroin addiction had been spreading so alarmingly throughout the country.

The Knapp Commission faced an extremely difficult choice. As a temporary commission, it had only limited ability to assemble evidence and the proof it had available to conduct public hearings into police corruption depended on a handful of witnesses, all with seamy backgrounds. Here was a witness who could tell inside stories about corruption in the most sensitive area of law enforcement. Chairman Whitman Knapp and Chief Counsel Michael Armstrong recognized the much more lasting benefits that could be realized if Leuci could be developed to work under cover over an extended period of time. The Knapp Commission would soon go out of business, so it offered to make Leuci available to the U. S. Attorney's office. Leuci, in turn, insisted that he would work only with the Federal prosecutor's office, which he felt he could trust.

The arrangement was quietly discussed at the top levels of the Department of Justice. Although police corruption itself is usually not a Federal crime, the possibility of developing obstruction of justice cases involving narcotics, or other criminal actions that come under Federal jurisdiction because of their interstate character, provided a sound basis for the Department's agreeing to take on the job. The U. S. Attorney's office undertook to provide major support for the project. Nicholas Scoppetta, who had won the confidence of Leuci, was quietly sworn in as a Special Assistant United States Attorney in the library-conference room with only a handful of members of the executive staff present. To avoid unnecessary inquiry, Mr. Scoppetta continued to work out of the offices of the Knapp Commission.

A new Official Corruption Unit was created in the U. S. Attorney's office. Edward M. Shaw, an experienced and skillful prosecutor who had handled many difficult cases, was named Executive Assistant U. S. Attorney and chief of the unit. Initially, investigators from the Knapp Commission, together with investigators from the U. S. Attorney's own staff, were used to follow Leuci when he held meetings with police officers, bondsmen, and lawyers. Each day, as he returned with new tape recordings, the extent of his contacts and the potential for unearthing corruption became more apparent.

The project gathered momentum. It was clear now that the corruption problem in New York City went far beyond the police and permeated virtually every aspect of the criminal justice system. Many outlaw policemen, bail bondsmen, defense attorneys, and prosecutors were flagrantly violating the law with little fear of being discovered. In narcotics enforcement the large sums of money available made corruption particularly attractive.

I met privately with Police Commissioner Patrick Murphy to discuss the project, and received a pledge of full cooperation and assistance. As the scope of Leuci's undercover work expanded, the need for additional manpower and funds became imperative. I asked the Bureau of Narcotics and Dangerous Drugs for assistance. First, I requested the loan of an automobile, then manpower, and, finally, a full investigative team.

Andrew Tartaglino, deputy director of BNDD, assumed direct responsibility for the agency's role in the project. A tough ex-policeman named Thomas Taylor was placed in immediate charge. A tight lid of security was put on the project. Only those who needed to know were told about it.

In the meantime, Police Commissioner Murphy had made available a special, handpicked squad of personnel from the Internal Affairs Division, who eventually set up offices away from police headquarters to avoid security leaks.

Emergencies developed almost every day during the undercover investigation. On several occasions Leuci's life was threatened. There were mishaps in surveillance and technical equipment. But progress was being made steadily. Leuci's contacts increased, as did the confidence of suspicious fellow officers.

One of the cases involved a private investigator who in turn became cooperating undercover operative for the U. S. Attorney's office. The private investigator told of patterns of corruption reaching into many of the courts in New York City. He agreed to help an undercover agent meet with a corrupt bondsman in Queens. So began the undercover investigation that ultimately led to the prosecution of Norman Archer, chief of the indictment bureau in the Queens County District Attorney's office. Slowly but surely, additional undercover personnel were introduced into the operation.

Meanwhile, a serious personal crisis had been developing for Leuci himself. The Knapp Commission had held its public hearings, and the counterattacks against the commission and its disclosures were intense. The Patrolmen's Benevolent Association attacked police officers who had testified in the hearing as traitors and turncoats. Leuci began to lose heart. He began to worry about the safety of his wife and children. He wondered what would happen to him once his undercover role had been revealed to the public. What would his former friends and colleagues in the police department think of him? What about disclosures of his own involvement in corrupt activities? The lawyers in the U. S. Attorney's office were only going to be there for a few years. He wanted to be in law enforcement for the rest of his life.

It was the low point in the entire investigation. Staff members working on the project held several agonizing conferences. They realized that Leuci's concerns were legitimate and they decided to do something about them. They arranged to move Leuci and his family to a new community and provide a twenty-four-hour guard to protect their lives. They made plans to ensure employment for Leuci as long as his cooperation continued. The most difficult problem of all, however, was how to overcome Leuci's concern about being regarded as a "traitor." The U. S. Attorney's staff kept assuring the detective that he was performing a hero's role in helping to bring an end to corruption in the administration of justice. But talk was not enough. Leuci was aware that in his own world he would be regarded as one who had betrayed his friends. So the staff started casting about for other ideas. They concluded that they should try to get a responsible journalist to write up Leuci's experiences and show the world that he had done courageous things in the interest of justice. The matter was discussed with the top people at BNDD, who suggested writers they thought they could trust not to publish information prejudicial to the investigation or to the rights of defendants. Someone mentioned Loudon Wainwright, one of the top reporters on *Life* magazine. If *Life* would write a personality profile on Leuci and tell about his experiences as an undercover agent, that would undoubtedly bolster his morale. More than that, it would also contribute to integrity in local law enforcement, by using Leuci as an example for police officers in other parts of the country of the type of courage it takes to combat bribery.

Mr. Wainwright was very much interested in doing the story and discussed it with his managing editor. A formal written agreement was signed between *Life* and the U. S. Attorney's office to avoid any possible misunderstanding. The problem was how to insure that the editorial control of the magazine and its own journalistic integrity were guaranteed, while at the same time assuring that no damage would be done to law enforcement objectives and due process requirements. An agreement between the U. S. Attorney's office and *Life* was finally concluded on April 7, 1972. It provided that *Life* would not publish anything until *after* indictments were filed, and that the U. S. Attorney's office would be given the opportunity to request (but not direct) the deletion of any material that would harm pending investigations or violate rules against prejudicial pretrial publicity. Otherwise full editorial control rested with the publisher.

The success of undercover operations depends entirely on the participants' not having any suspicion that they are dealing with persons cooperating with the Federal Government. As more and more undercover inquiries got under way, concerns about possible disclosure of the investigations grew.

In mid-May, David Burnham of the *Times* phoned and told me that he knew the identity of the main undercover agent who was working with the Federal Government in its corruption investigation. Burnham said that he was aware of the importance of the work that was going on. I asked him not to publish whatever information he had for the time being because it would jeopardize ongoing investigations and obviously risk harm to the agent himself. Burnham said that he wanted to discuss the matter in person and made an appointment to come in to the office.

On June 1, 1972, David Burnham conferred with several of us. Burnham said that he did not intend to publish a story immediately because he was aware that if he did so the story could result in Leuci's being killed. I advised Burnham that any publication about the investigation would be extremely harmful to ongoing projects. Because of Burnham's role from the outset in the police-corruption investigation, I said, the office would be willing to brief him on the progress that had been made, but only on the condition that he would not publish anything until the investigation had been completed. In a spirit of fairness, I volunteered to Burnham that a similar arrangement had been entered into with *Life* magazine, which was preparing a biographical profile on the undercover agent and the nature of his investigative work. At this point Burnham suddenly became visibly annoyed and asked why the *Life* arrangement had been made. The reasons were briefly explained to him. Somewhat mollified, Burnham then said he would discuss the whole matter with his editor and would try to arrange for a conference between me and his editor at the *Times* to discuss it. He tentatively set the date of Thursday, June 8, for such a meeting.

June 8 came and went with no word from Burnham. Then abruptly, at 4:50 P.M. on Wednesday, June 14, Burnham phoned and advised me that he had discussed with his editors the request not to publish information about the investigation until it had been completed and they had decided to go ahead with publication. In fact, he added, he was working on a story right then.

I immediately called A. M. Rosenthal, managing editor of the *Times*, and requested a meeting at the earliest available opportunity. I wanted to brief Rosenthal on the importance of the investigations so he could assess the importance of holding off public disclosure until the investigations had run their course. Rosenthal said that he would discuss the request with his colleagues but that he was doubtful that such a meeting would be useful. The conversation ended shortly after five, with the seven o'clock deadline for the first edition of the following morning's *Times* just two hours away. Rosenthal did not call back for more than an hour. Finally, at 6:10 P.M., he told me that he had discussed the matter with his associates and that they had decided to go ahead and publish the story, and in fact were going to do so that very evening. When I asked Rosenthal why he would not at least hold up the story long enough to hear the facts, Rosenthal responded, "Bay of Pigs." He went on to explain that he had learned from the Bay of Pigs experience that it was better to go ahead with the story once you have the information than to delay publishing it. I said I was not attempting to interfere with the paper's editorial freedom but simply to insure that the editors were adequately informed about the facts so that after publication, if they still decided to go forward, they would not say, "Why didn't you tell us before?" Rosenthal's answer was still No.

In the meantime, Andrew Tartaglino, at the BNDD office in Washington, was also having his problems in trying to prevent disclosure. William Federici, a *Daily News* reporter, had obtained a tip about Leuci from police headquarters in New York and planned to publish a story about what he knew. Tartaglino, having been assured by his own public information officer that Federici was a responsible reporter, then offered to brief him *off the record* in return for a promise not to publish until after the indictments were filed. Federici agreed, and Tartaglino then supplied him with detailed information concerning ten major undercover investigations that were then in progress. It was a fatal mistake.

When *The New York Times* city edition hit the streets, shortly before midnight on June 14, the staff at the *Daily News* was outraged. The managing editor there knew that Federici had the complete story and had committed himself not to publish it. Moreover, he had had the story for several weeks. Now the *Times* had scooped the *News*. The city desk got Federici on the phone. He dictated a short story in time for the late city editions.

On the following morning, the *Times* carried a front-page story with David Burnham's by-line.

U.S. LOOKING INTO HEROIN BRIBERY HERE:
SOME OFFICIALS ARE SAID TO BE IMPLICATED

Burnham specifically named Leuci, who was at that very moment conducting an undercover investigation.

For more than a year, wearing a tiny radio transmitter in his belt and driving a tan two-door Pontiac equipped with an elaborate system of hidden microphones, Detective Leuci has been collecting evidence for a special investigation team established in the early spring of 1971 by United States Attorney Whitney North Seymour, Jr.

Not to be outdone, the *Daily News* had its own story:

ELITE COPS & LAWYERS IN DOPE FIX QUIZ

A forlorn group of Federal prosecutors and investigators assembled in the U. S. Attorney's conference room that morning with crumpled copies of the *Times* and *News* in their hands. They conferred for several hours trying to assess the damage and decide what steps could be taken to salvage some of the cases. Several staff members expressed the hope that the investigations into judicial corruption, which did not involve narcotics cases, might still be safe. As to the police-corruption aspects of the investigation, however, it was clear that no further evidence could be obtained from those with whom Leuci had been dealing. We devised an emergency program. Before the policemen began to exchange information with each other, the investigators reasoned, the Federal prosecutors would confront them with the evidence, and try to enlist their aid in further investigations. A team of ten Assistant U. S. Attorneys was enlisted and briefed. Federal narcotics agents and police department IAD personnel invited the ten most likely candidates for cooperation to meet with the Assistant U. S. Attorneys in rooms in a midtown hotel. Buoyed by hopes of salvaging at least some of the fifteen months' effort, the team divided up their assignments, studied the cases against each of the policemen, and adjourned for supper in preparation for a major roundup early the following morning.

But Burnham's destructive action had not yet run its course. The *News* was still incensed at the *Times'* scoop. When the first edition of the following day's *Daily News* hit the stands, there was a comprehensive, detailed story by William Federici, spelling out the details of every one of the major ongoing undercover operations, supplied to him off the record by Tartaglino.

All hope of continuing the undercover investigations was destroyed. Nothing remained to be done but to move immediately to try to wind up the few cases that had been partially completed. A team of Assistant U. S. Attorneys worked through the night drafting search warrants, interviewing witnesses, and making preparations to collect final bits of evidence the following morning. By 6 A.M, two Assistant U. S. Attorneys and a host of BNDD agents appeared before Magistrate Max Schiffman in the Eastern District of New York, requesting the issuance of search warrants. Other staff members reported to the midtown hotel for the roundup of corrupt police officers. (In one of those odd twists of fate, that effort proved to be almost totally wasted. When Federal investigators went to the addresses listed for the police officers on their official personnel records, they found that the addresses were false. Most officers lived outside of the city but had given bogus N.Y.C. addresses for official purposes.)

The investigation was now finished. For the sake of a scoop, the *Times* had destroyed it. Now the question was what, if anything, to do about it.

No one in public life relishes the thought of a fight with the press. Journalists have long memories. The tradition of independence of the Southern District of New York nonetheless began to take command. "We have always stood up against adversaries to fight for what was right," said one staff member. "Why don't we have the guts to stand against the press, too?"

A press conference was called on June 21, 1972, exactly one week after the futile attempts to persuade the *Times* editors to hold off identifying Robert Leuci until the investigations were completed. As U. S. Attorney, I told the assembled reporters:

> The public should be fully aware that there is no reasonable expectation that any significant number of indictments can now be expected. Regrettably the public

must accept the fact that a number of public officials as to whom serious questions of integrity have been raised will continue to hold positions of trust because our effort to develop evidence has been aborted by these premature disclosures.

Then came an appeal to the news media to exercise responsible judgment on behalf of the public interest.

> What conceivable end was served by these damaging disclosures? How could the public be benefited by cutting off these investigations?
>
> Under our Constitution, the press is guaranteed absolute freedom to exercise its own judgment as to what to publish and what not to publish. Government has no power to interfere with those judgments, but the press does.
>
> Our office will now try to pick up the pieces of this investigation and see whether any parts of it can be salvaged. That is our public duty.
>
> We suggest that the editors of the newspapers involved pick up the pieces of their obligation to the people of New York and see whether any parts of it can be salvaged. They, too, have a public duty.

The reaction was predictable. The press closed ranks and counterattacked the U. S. Attorney's office. They seized on the arrangement with *Life* magazine and accused the Federal prosecutors of trying to "manage the news." The argument, of course, was a total twisting of the truth. *Life* had not been given details of any investigations but only an opportunity to write a personality profile and description of the work of the undercover agent. More than that, the *Life* editors firmly bound themselves not to publish until *after* the indictments had been returned. They had abided by that agreement, unlike the *Times* and the *News*. That was the crucial difference.

12

THE FUTURE OF FEDERAL LAW ENFORCEMENT

On June 15, 1971, United States Attorneys from all parts of the country filed into the seats of the FBI auditorium in the Department of Justice building in Washington to hear a talk by the Deputy Attorney General of the United States. Richard G. Kleindienst radiated confidence and good humor as he rose to his feet to address the country's top Federal law enforcement officers. He quipped about the political climate in the nation's capital as the election year of 1972 approached. With a broad smile he joked about the party slogans that were currently being circulated around town. The Republican slogan, he said, was this: "It took us ten years to get this country away from the people, and we're not going to give it back without a fight!"

His audience laughed with him. Then Kleindienst turned deadly serious. "It is of utmost importance to keep this Administration in power," he said, "and you men must do everything you can to insure that result." It was a theme that Mr. Kleindienst would repeat again and again in meetings with U. S. Attorneys over the coming months. His listeners were instructed to call attention to the law-and-order achievements of Mr. Nixon and his Administration and avoid controversies that might lose votes. It was only a glimmer, but the partisan political orientation of the Attorney General's office was beginning to show through.

On the pediment of the Supreme Court Building in Washington, D.C., are chiseled the words EQUAL JUSTICE UNDER LAW. This is the fundamental concept on which Federal law enforcement is built. But there are many flaws in its implementation, which should not be tolerated. We need to reshape our thinking about the role of Federal law enforcement agencies and Federal prosecutors, the structure in which they function, and the goals toward which they work.

In the broadest terms, future reforms in Federal law enforcement must seek to eliminate inappropriate use of criminal sanctions; to develop better alternatives to traditional criminal prosecution; to guarantee fair play in judicial due process for all, regardless of circumstances or wealth; and to focus our concept of corrections on salvaging human beings for more constructive lives.

The traditional concept of the prosecutor as a public lawyer who merely presents evidence, questions witnesses, and seeks prison sentences is out of step with today's world. The prosecutor's primary obligation should be creative use of all available law enforcement resources to protect the public against antisocial conduct; to protect the individual citizen in his Constitutional rights; to ensure that the laws providing new government benefits are properly implemented; and to contribute affirmatively to integrity in government and constructive moral leadership for the community.

Federal law enforcement has outgrown its ability to meet its responsibilities fairly and effectively. The abuses of power, invasion of rights, and obstruction of justice recently demonstrated by those at the highest levels of the Government have plainly shown that strong measures are needed to insulate the enforcement of the law from political partisanship and lawless official conduct.

REMOVING LAW ENFORCEMENT FROM POLITICAL CONTROL

We must give highest priority to eliminating political interference with law enforcement. This requires positive steps to remove two inherent defects from the present Federal law enforcement structure. Both of them undercut the goal of impartial, evenhanded enforcement of Federal law:

First, we must isolate those functions of the Department of Justice and the Federal Bureau of Investigation which require primary loyalty to the Administration in power, and separate them from those functions that should be characterized by unwavering objectivity and impartiality.

Second, we must remove the selection of principal law enforcement officials from the arena of partisan politics.

1. *Separation of Functions*

The most serious problem in the present Department of Justice is that the Attorney General has a built-in conflict of interest which permeates much of the Department's operation and spills over into the Federal Bureau of Investigation. This is not simply a problem of character and personality which can be corrected by picking a different man for the job. It reflects a fundamental flaw in the original conception of the Department of Justice, and unless that flaw is corrected, we will never solve the underlying problem.

The dilemma is that we expect the Attorney General to serve two masters at the same time: one is the President, to whom he reports, as personal and political adviser; the other is the ideal of nonpartisan, evenhanded Justice. Time and time again, these two functions collide with each other head-on. Whenever it would be politically embarrassing to the President to have some particular investigation or prosecution instituted or pursued, the conflict of interest immediately comes into play. Whenever questions involving policy matters within the jurisdiction of the Department—such as internal security, antitrust policy, or enforcement of civil rights statutes—require advice to the President from both a political and a legal point of view, the conflict of interest reappears. Loyalty to the political interests of the Administration may often require disloyalty to the goal of impartial justice.

There is only one way to put an end to this built-in conflict— by creating two distinct senior executive positions with different loyalties and different functions. In deference to historical tradition, one might still be called "Attorney General." The other might be called "Chief Prosecutor." Other labels would do as well. In England, the political adviser has been known over the course of history as the Chancellor, while the chief prosecuting officer has been known as Attorney General. In Sweden, there is a Minister of Justice, selected by the party in power, and then both an Attorney General and a Chief Crown Prosecutor, who are civil servants. The important thing is not the label but the function.

The presidential adviser should logically be responsible for the following offices now in the Department of Justice, all of which are intimately involved with the policy interests of the Administration: the Office of Legal Counsel; Office of Legislative Affairs; Community Relations Service; Law Enforcement Assistance Administration; and, possibly, the Immigration and Naturalization Service (which more properly belongs in a manpower agency). He could also be vested with formulating broad enforcement policy.

The Chief Prosecutor should have a separate and distinct law enforcement agency under his direction (possibly a "Federal Law Enforcement Agency"), which would cover all of the existing civil and criminal litigation and law enforcement functions in the Department of Justice, including specifically the Criminal, Civil, Tax, Civil Rights, Antitrust, and Land and Natural Resources divisions. The Solicitor General and Pardon Attorney should also be part of such agency, as should the principal investigative agencies. (The Bureau of Prisons, however, should be elsewhere—in an agency concerned with human resources, such as HEW, rather than one concerned with prosecutions.) Internal security matters should be entirely removed from the law enforcement sphere, except for specific violations of criminal statutes which are nonpolitical in nature.

The Chief Prosecutor and the agency under him should have no direct working relationships with the White House. For broad enforcement policy-making purposes, he probably should be made answerable to the Attorney General, but not in the handling of individual cases. The office should be totally independent in specific investigations and litigation. To this extent, the concept of a Chief Prosecutor is very similar to the proposal frequently advanced for the creation of a permanent "Special Prosecutor." The difference is that the Chief Prosecutor would have much broader powers and his enforcement responsibilities would be more deeply institutionalized in relation to other law enforcement agencies.

These same lines of division should also apply to the Federal Bureau of Investigation. It, too, suffers from an internal conflict of interest. To the extent that the FBI is engaged in internal security work and background checks on the qualifications of prospective presidential appointees, its primary loyalty is directly to the White House. On the other hand, when it comes to investigation and enforcement of the Federal laws, particularly Federal crimes, the work of the FBI should be completely impersonal and objective and should not be subject to any interference from the President or members of the White House staff.

In one of the last annual reports of FBI activity submitted by J. Edgar Hoover, a substantial portion was taken up with listing the public appearances of Communist Party leaders at student meetings on various college campuses. Another lengthy section of the report listed speaking appearances by Black Panther representatives at institutions, including both colleges and high schools. Unquestionably, these are matters of interest to those who are concerned with the political atmosphere in the nation, and undoubtedly intelligence operations about mass meetings and threats of disruption of government are of importance to the appropriate governmental agencies. But they are not comparable functions to criminal investigation. To use the same regulations, same supervision, same answerability, and essentially the same personnel to perform both functions is unwise and unhealthy. The image of the FBI in recent years has been injured by the appearance of preoccupation with political persecution. This has been most unfortunate in terms of public confidence in the impartial administration of justice. The Wounded Knee, Berrigan brothers, and Camden Draft Board cases have all produced damaging evidence of improper conduct by FBI-supervised undercover operatives.

In November, 1974, Attorney General William B. Saxbe disclosed that the FBI had been engaged in secret counter-intelligence operations, known as "Cointelpro," which involved organizing disruptive activities against political groups, including such civil rights organizations as the Student Nonviolent Coordinating Committee, the Southern Christian Leadership Conference, and the Congress of Racial Equality. Between 1956 and 1971, a total of 2,370 disruptive operations were implemented by the Bureau, some of which utilized techniques described by Assistant Attorney General Henry E. Petersen as "abhorrent in a free society." These counterintelligence activities were apparently carried out without even informing some of the Attorneys General in office at the time.

Is it really sound for the largest investigative agency in the nation to be engaged in this type of covert activity? Can an agency that engages in "abhorrent" conduct be expected to respect the Constitutional rights of individuals in criminal investigations? Would it not be more sensible to use the immense resources of the FBI to deal with problems of criminal justice and law enforcement, and leave national security intelligence-gathering to others?

We have recently seen the tragic results that flow from combining dual loyalties in the Director of the FBI. In order to please the White House, the Director has willingly made false public statements about the use of FBI personnel to investigate newsmen; has destroyed incriminating evidence; and has taken secret-police type action to block staff access to the offices of the Attorney General and Special Prosecutor. These three examples involved three different Directors of the FBI. Yet each one of them constituted a perversion of the proper role for the head of an objective, impartial law enforcement agency.

There is only one sure remedy: the functions of the FBI should be split up, and those operations concerned with national security and related matters should be placed in one agency and those concerned with objective fact-gathering and impartial law enforcement in another. The head of one agency might be called the "Director of Security," and the other "Director of Investigations." They should never again be one and the same man.

2. Selection of Law Enforcement Officials

Once the concept of separating these two conflicting functions is recognized and implemented, the next step is to work out a process of selection which will insulate the Chief Prosecutor and the Director of Investigations from the political arena. One possible solution would be to establish a nominating commission that would be required to compile, when there was a vacancy in one of these offices, a brief list of the best-qualified candidates, from which the President or Attorney General would be required to make a selection, subject to Senate confirmation.

The creation of a nonpolitical nominating commission should also be considered as a means of achieving merit selection of United States Attorneys. Each United States Attorney was originally vested with complete authority to handle Federal criminal and civil matters in his district. He was not subject to any supervision by the Attorney General until the establishment of the Department of Justice, in 1870. Subsequent legislation has now given increasing control to the Attorney General. In civil rights, internal security and election fraud matters, this control is absolute. Properly, the United States Attorneys should be under the supervision of a nonpolitical chief prosecutor; not under the direction of a political adviser to the President. That does not mean, however, that these officials should not be finally selected by the President or by the Attorney General, to give them a stature in keeping with the importance of the office. However, the existing practices in selecting candidates for United States Attorney have been excessively partisan and political. This partisanship has frequently interfered with the independence and effectiveness of the office.

Political independence for United States Attorneys could be achieved by the establishment of a circuit nominating commission in each judicial circuit of the United States, with responsibility for nominating candidates for United States Attorney and United States district and circuit judges in that circuit. Such a commission should be nonpartisan and broadly based; the chief judge in each district court might select one member of the commission, the chief judge of the circuit court might select three members, and additional members might be selected by the bar associations or Governors of the affected states. Such nominating commissions would be obligated to collect the names of potential candidates, to conduct full investigations of their qualifications, and then to submit a list of the best-qualified candidates to the President for his selection. The name of the candidate would only then be submitted to the Senate for confirmation. This kind of approach—which has been employed successfully for the merit selection of judges—would preserve the answerability of elected public officials for the appointment of senior executive and judicial officers, while at the same time effectively removing the selection process from partisan politics.

When it comes to selection of the Chief Prosecutor and the Director of Investigations, a national nominating commission might be constituted, to be made up of the heads of the various circuit nominating commissions plus a chairman to be appointed by the Chief Justice. This body would then submit the names of nominees from which the President would choose these Federal officials.

Obviously, it is desirable to fix a term of office for the Chief Prosecutor and Director of Investigations. Five or six years, to insure some overlap, would appear to be about right.

As for the official who remains as political adviser to the President, whether he be called Attorney General, Chancellor, Minister of Justice, or whatever, selection should be left to the present method, under which the President chooses those officials who will directly carry out his Administration's policies. The same could be true for the Director of Security, who would still be subject to congressional review at budget time. The important thing is to deprive these officials of direct supervision over the case-by-case enforcement of Federal laws. Law enforcement in particular cases should have no involvement with political considerations.

BETTER MANAGEMENT PRACTICES

Like all large government agencies, the Department of Justice has grown into a sprawling mass of miscellaneous bureaus and agencies. There are now nearly fifty thousand employees in the Department, of whom only 6½ percent are lawyers. Lawyers still run the Department, and run it badly. Basic reforms in personnel policies and operating procedures are critically needed.

The Department

Among the most pressing management changes are these:

1. Executive staff quality must be strengthened at the echelon just below the Assistant Attorneys General, where most management decisions (or, more correctly, indecisions) take place, and particular emphasis should be placed on initiative and responsibility.

2. Efficient management techniques must be instituted to control the movement of files, correspondence, and other items requiring action or decisions, with workable "tickler" procedures and follow-up.

3. A departmental ombudsman should be established to serve as troubleshooter, to handle inquiries into incompetence or misconduct, and to cut through red tape and delays in the day-to-day functioning of the agency.

4. Standard procedures to protect prosecutive integrity should be established to insure that there is no discussion of pending matters with outsiders unless the staff attorney in charge of the matter is present, and to guarantee proper record-keeping on all inquiries from Congress or elsewhere, so that the impartiality of the law enforcement function will be above suspicion.

U. S. Attorneys' Offices

In the field operations of the Department carried out through the local United States Attorneys, additional changes are urgently needed:

1. Standard staff-recruiting and interview procedures should be established to protect against political influence or inter-

ference in the hiring of Assistant U. S. Attorneys, and to insure that job opportunities are available to all qualified young lawyers strictly on the basis of merit.

2. A limited permanent cadre of career lawyers (in a ratio of about one-to-ten) should be selected from experienced Assistants who have served at least five years, to insure continuity and to avoid waste motion, with good pay and attractive pension benefits.

3. Regular staff positions should be established for qualified "research assistants" to supplement lawyers and criminal investigators in collecting evidence in such new law enforcement fields as consumer protection, equal employment opportunities, housing, health care, welfare, and many other specialized areas.

4. Paralegal personnel should also become a standard part of the U. S. Attorney's staff to handle administrative problems with case control, voluminous exhibits, detention records, and operational studies.

5. Criminal investigation resources should be much more closely coordinated with the prosecutor's office through (a) the creation of a small in-house investigative staff to handle emergency matters and highly sensitive investigations, and (b) a reorientation of Federal investigative agency operations to insure direct assistance, as needed, on all official investigations instituted by the U. S. Attorney.

6. Fiscal responsibility for expenses having a direct impact on investigations or prosecutions (such as witness travel, expert testimony, and undercover operations) should be under the direct control of law enforcement, rather than administrative, personnel.

USE OF CIVIL ENFORCEMENT TECHNIQUES

The rigidity and complexity of using criminal law to control antisocial conduct have clogged the courts and dissipated law enforcement resources. Much more use should be made of the injunction, civil commitment, monetary penalties, and judicial censure as sanctions to prevent violations, particularly in such areas as consumer abuse, fraud, business regulation, deprivation of rights, and environmental protection.

There are many benefits for all concerned in using the civil side of the court for enforcement purposes. Federal civil procedure provides full discovery for both sides and permits quick court action where there is no real dispute over the facts, through applications for preliminary injunctions and for summary judgment. In civil proceedings the prosecutor can prove his case by a preponderance of the evidence rather than by the much more rigid standard of "beyond a reasonable doubt." This means less time spent searching for peripheral witnesses and preparing technical proof. Where equitable remedies are needed, such as an injunction or an accounting, the time-consuming jury process is avoided, since these matters are presented to the court alone. Civil procedures also permit the use of special masters and magistrates to supervise pre-trial motions and hearings and thereby greatly expand the courts' capacity to handle a high volume of complicated matters. If, therefore, a civil remedy can be at least as effective as a criminal penalty, the civil side of the court provides an unusually good vehicle for achieving desirable law enforcement results.

STRATEGIC PLANNING FOR FEDERAL LAW ENFORCEMENT

The one overriding defect in Federal law enforcement is the lack of any meaningful coordination in the use of enforcement resources. Policy-making on the national level is nonexistent in most areas of criminal justice. Individual United States Attorneys are allowed to set their own enforcement policy in important and sensitive fields. Although a certain amount of free enterprise is desirable to help generate new ideas and test out new concepts, as a matter of long-range operations, studied anarchy is not desirable in Federal law enforcement. The wide differences in the types of cases prosecuted in different Federal districts (see Chapter Two), and the wide range of sentencing policies as applied by the courts, clearly demonstrate the need for better coordination. By repeating expensive lessons on a district-by-district basis, we waste precious resources—not to mention violating the concept of evenhanded justice.

Federal and state law enforcement could be dramatically strengthened by the creation of a "National Law Enforcement Planning Council," similar to the Council of Economic Advisers, to report each year to the President on the state of crime and law enforcement and to recommend the proper allocation of human and fiscal resources. The council should propose a national enforcement policy in such fields as, for example, illegal gambling, and should explore the most effective way for dealing with the *real* abuses from such activities—in the case of gambling, the siphoning of huge amounts of untaxed dollars into the hands of organized crime. Instead of leaving gambling enforcement in its present sporadic state, dependent entirely on the interest of prosecutors in particular districts, the council should establish national enforcement goals and policies, pool intelligence, and exchange practical experience on effective law enforcement techniques. Existing resources can and should be used much more effectively and economically.

Some of the areas that need national law enforcement planning include consumer fraud, misuse of secret foreign bank accounts, corruption in the administration of justice, urban-renewal frauds, election law abuses, narcotics distribution, pollution control enforcement, hijacking, employment discrimination, and improper delivery of government-funded programs and services. The goal is to pool experience and insight into law enforcement problems, with participation from specialists and technicians other than prosecutors and investigators.

The National Law Enforcement Planning Council should provide policy directions for the new Chief Prosecutor. Representatives of the United States Attorneys in the field should participate actively in the council's work, as should representatives of state and local agencies. Experts from other fields should also participate, including economists, planners, scientists, sociologists, and others who can make significant contributions to sound law enforcement planning.

We have lived through a period of extreme challenge to the governmental structure of this nation. The Federal law enforcement machinery and the Federal courts have been severely tested. On the whole, despite betrayals of trust by officials at the highest level, the institutions have survived and proved their worth. Out of the experience has come a clearer perception of what is wrong with Federal law enforcement and what needs to be done to make it strong. The ultimate goal is a simple one, integrity—the ability of the Federal law enforcement establishment to act fairly and firmly, with decency, impartiality, and independence. The secret of achieving it was articulated by former United States Attorney Henry L. Stimson, at the age of eighty, as he looked back over a career dedicated to public service.

> The sinfulness and weakness of man are evident to anyone who lives in the active world. But men are also good and great, kind and wise. Honor begets honor; trust begets trust; faith begets faith; and hope is the mainspring of life. . . . The man who tries to work for the good, believing in its eventual victory, while he may suffer setback and even disaster, will never know defeat. The only deadly sin I know is cynicism.

APPENDIX

Assistant United States Attorneys who served under Whitney North Seymour, Jr., in the Southern District of New York.

Taggart D. Adams
Harold Baer, Jr.
Eugene F. Bannigan
Mel P. Barkan
Richard Ben-Veniste
David M. Brodsky
William R. Bronner
John N. Bush
H. Thomas Coghill
John P. Cooney, Jr.
Joseph D. Danas
Richard J. Davis
V. Pamela Davis
Peter R. De Filippi
John H. Doyle III
Douglas F. Eaton
Alvin W. Fargo, III
Gerald A. Feffer
Kenneth R. Feinberg
Lawrence S. Feld
Nicholas Figueroa
Thomas Fitzpatrick

Susan Freiman
Brian J. Gallagher
William J. Gilbreth
Rudolph W. Giuliani
Richard A. Givens
Steven J. Glassman
John D. Gordan III
William B. Gray
John H. Gross
Richard M. Hall
Jeffrey Harris
Joel B. Harris
Robert T. Hartmann
Dennis J. Helms
Robert B. Hemley
Peter A. Herbert
Michael D. Hess
Walter J. Higgins, Jr.
Jay S. Horowitz
Patricia M. Hynes
Joseph Jaffe
Sterling Johnson, Jr.

Robert M. Jupiter
Jack Kaplan
David V. Keegan
John J. Kelleher
John J. Kenney
Edward J. Kuriansky
David P. Land
Carter La Prade
James P. Lavin
Bobby C. Lawyer
Bancroft Littlefield, Jr.
John A. Lowe
David A. Luttinger
William Cullen
    MacDonald
Andrew J. Maloney
Joseph P. Marro
Maurice M. McDermott
Harold F. McGuire, Jr.
John F. McHugh
M. Blane Michael
Silvio J. Mollo

240

Alan B. Morrison
Robert G. Morvillo
Michael B. Mukasey
Arthur A. Munisteri
Daniel H. Murphy, II
Gary P. Naftalis
Shirah Neiman
James E. Nesland
John W. Nields, Jr.
David Paget
Walter M. Phillips, Jr.
Henry Putzel, III
Jed S. Rakoff
James W. Rayhill
Naomi L. Reice
T. Gorman Reilly
Peter F. Rient
Daniel Riesel
Dean C. Rohrer
Christopher du Pont
    Roosevelt

Gerald A. Rosenberg
Yale L. Rosenberg
Barbara Ann Rowan
Walter S. Rowland
John C. Sabetta
Elliot G. Sagor
Jon A. Sale
Michael I. Saltzman
Ross Sandler
S. Andrew Schaffer
James Schreiber
Bart M. Schwartz
Nicholas Scoppetta
Edward M. Shaw
Milton Sherman
Anne Sidamon-Eristoff
Michael C. Silberberg
Paul H. Silverman
Ira L. Sorkin
Daniel J. Sullivan
Howard S. Sussman

William M. Tendy
James P. Tierney
John J. Tigue, Jr.
Richard S. Toder
James T. B. Tripp
Peter L. Truebner
Allan A. Tuttle
Charles B. Updike
Franklin B. Velie
Arthur J. Viviani
John M. Walker, Jr.
Stanley H. Wallenstein
Robert P. Walton
George E. Wilson
Howard Wilson
Samuel J. Wilson
John R. Wing
Frank H. Wohl
Dennison Young, Jr.

INDEX

243

INDEX